SAXON MATH™
Course 3

Standards Success

Common Core State Standards Companion
for use with *Saxon Math Course 3*

SAXON®

HOUGHTON MIFFLIN HARCOURT

Printed in the U.S.A.

ISBN 978-0-547-50712-5

4 5 6 7   0304   19 18 17 16

4500592470   A B C D E F G

Table of Contents

Correlation of *Saxon Math Course 3* to the Common Core State Standards for Mathematics Grade 8

Standards for Mathematical Practice – *This standard is covered throughout the program; the following are examples.*

1. Make sense of problems and persevere in solving them.	**Power Up:** PS1, PU2, PU8, PS12, PU13, PU23, PS23, PS35, PU40, PU45, PS45, PU49, PU53, PS53, PU56, PU58, PS64, PU70, PS76, PU83, PS83, PS92, PU85, PU98, PS102, PS115 **Lessons:** L3, WP3, L4, WP4, WP5, WP6, WP7, WP18, L34, WP37, WP39, WP40, L45, L49, WP52, L53, L58, L70, Inv7, WP76, L87, WP87, L89, WP90, WP91, WP94, Inv10, L105, WP105, WP106, WP108 **Other:** SFA 16
2. Reason abstractly and quantitatively.	**Power Up:** PS12, PS15, PS17, PS25, PS37, PS45, PS54, PS61, PS72, PS79, PS94, PS99, PS109, PS118 **Lessons:** L3, L4, L17, WP17, WP21, WP24, WP26, L38, L45, L49, L58, L59, WP59, Inv7, L87, L89, WP89, Inv9, WP93 **Other:** SFA6, SFA14, SFA20
3. Construct viable arguments and critique the reasoning of others.	**Power Up:** PS1, PS15, PS25, PS36, PS49, PS68, PS79, PS96, PS109 **Lessons:** L3, L9, L17, WP18, L19, WP19, L20, WP21, WP22, WP26, WP29, WP35, L35, L59, Inv7, Inv8, WP84, Inv9, L113, L116, Inv12 **Other:** SFA5
4. Model with mathematics.	**Power Up:** PS6, PS9, PS11, PS22, PS26, PS34, PS59, PS74, PS84, PS92, PS113 **Lessons:** WP6, L9, L10, WP10, Inv1, L22, L26, WP27, L31, L33, L34, WP34, WP36, Inv4, L41, WP41, WP43, WP45, Inv5, L49, L55, WP64, WP66, L68, L75, Inv8, WP108 **Other:** SFA15, SFA19, SFA23, SFA28
5. Use appropriate tools strategically.	**Lessons:** L16, L18, Inv2, L28, L30, WP39, WP43, L51, Inv7, L73, WP76, Inv10 **Other:** SFA10
6. Attend to precision.	**Power Up:** PU1, PU4, PU6, PU8, PU10, PU18, PU32, PS32, PU38, PU42, PU49, PU61, PU79, PU95 **Lessons:** LP17, WP17, LP28, WP28, LP30, WP30, LP39, WP39, L40, WP40, L78, WP78, L0103, WP103, L117 **Other:** SFA8, SFA9, SFA13
7. Look for and make use of structure.	**Lessons:** L2, L3, L4, WP4, WP5, WP7, WP9, Inv2, L21, WP21, WP23, WP26, L30, L31, L33, L35, L38, L51, L61, L70, L73, WP73, WP74, L97, L102, **Other:** SFA11, SFA24, SFA27
8. Look for and express regularity in repeated reasoning.	**Power Up:** PS26, PS37, PS40, PS42, PS44, PS48, PS51, PS59, PS103, PS107, PS111, PS116 **Lessons:** L9, L15, L21, WP22, WP23, WP26, L28, WP29, L34, L44, L45, L48, L61, L67, L70, L73, L75, WP73, WP74, WP76, Inv8, L83, L88, L92, L97, WP97, WP98, Inv10, L102, WP102, WP108 **Other:** SFA2

COMMON CORE Common Core State Standards	*Saxon Math Course 3 Citations* *References in italics indicate foundational.*

The Number System 8.NS

Know that there are numbers that are not rational, and approximate them by rational numbers.

1. Understand informally that every number has a decimal expansion; the rational numbers are those with decimal expansions that terminate in 0s or eventually repeat. Know that other numbers are called irrational.	**Power Up:** PS89 **Lessons:** L12, WP12, L16, WP16, WP18, WP19, WP20, L30, WP30, WP31, WP32, WP35, WP39, WP43, WP47, WP50, WP56, L63, WP63, WP81 **Other:** GC3, SFA4

Key: **Inv:** Investigation   **PS:** Problem Solving   **SFA:** Standards Focus Activity
       L: Lesson   **PU:** Power Up   **WP:** Written Practice

2. Use rational approximations of irrational numbers to compare the size of irrational numbers, locate them approximately on a number line diagram, and estimate the value of expressions (e.g., π^2).	**Power Up:** PS31, PU31 **Lessons:** L16, WP18, WP19, WP20, L66, WP78, WP81 **Other:** SFA2

Expressions and Equations 8.EE

Work with radicals and integer exponents.

1. Know and apply the properties of integer exponents to generate equivalent numerical expressions.	**Power Up:** PU16, PU17, PU19, PU31, PS62, PU62, PU64, PU66, PU72, PU86, PU96, PU100 **Lessons:** L15, WP15, Inv2, WP25, L27, WP28, WP29, WP30, WP31, WP32, WP33, WP34, WP41, L51, L57 **Other:** SFA1
2. Use square root and cube root symbols to represent solutions to equations of the form $x^2 = p$ and $x^3 = p$, where p is a positive rational number. Evaluate square roots of small perfect squares and cube roots of small perfect cubes. Know that $\sqrt{2}$ is irrational.	**Lessons:** L15, L16, WP16, WP17, Inv2, L66, WP85, L93, WP93, WP96, WP98, WP102, WP105, WP107, WP111, WP112, WP115 **Other:** GC16, SFA19
3. Use numbers expressed in the form of a single digit times an integer power of 10 to estimate very large or very small quantities, and to express how many times as much one is than the other.	**Lessons:** L28, WP30, WP31, WP34, WP39, L46, WP47, L51, WP52, WP53, WP55, WP56, L57, WP58, WP59, WP99 **Other:** GC6, GC11, SFA12
4. Perform operations with numbers expressed in scientific notation, including problems where both decimal and scientific notation are used. Use scientific notation and choose units of appropriate size for measurements of very large or very small quantities (e.g., use millimeters per year for seafloor spreading). Interpret scientific notation that has been generated by technology.	**Lessons:** L28, WP30, WP31, WP34, WP39, L46, WP47, L51, WP52, WP53, WP55, WP56, L57, WP58, WP59, WP60, WP99 **Other:** GC6, GC11, SFA10

Understand the connections between proportional relationships, lines, and linear equations.

5. Graph proportional relationships, interpreting the unit rate as the slope of the graph. Compare two different proportional relationships represented in different ways.	**Lessons:** L41, L44, WP47, WP48, WP49, L69, WP77, L88, WP88 **Other:** SFA15
6. Use similar triangles to explain why the slope m is the same between any two distinct points on a non-vertical line in the coordinate plane; derive the equation $y = mx$ for a line through the origin and the equation $y = mx + b$ for a line intercepting the vertical axis at b.	**Lessons:** L56 **Other:** SFA28

Analyze and solve linear equations and pairs of simultaneous linear equations.

7. Solve linear equations in one variable.	
a. Give examples of linear equations in one variable with one solution, infinitely many solutions, or no solutions. Show which of these possibilities is the case by successively transforming the given equation into simpler forms, until an equivalent equation of the form $x = a$, $a = a$, or $a = b$ results (where a and b are different numbers).	**Lessons:** L14, WP14, WP15, WP16, WP17, WP18, WP19, WP20, WP21, WP23, WP46, WP57 **Other:** SFA7

Saxon Math Course 3

b. Solve linear equations with rational number coefficients, including equations whose solutions require expanding expressions using the distributive property and collecting like terms.	**Lessons:** L38, L50, WP50, WP51, WP52, WP54, WP55, L56, WP56, WP57, WP58, WP61, WP62, WP64, WP66, WP69, LA61, LA62, LA63, LA64, LA65 **Other:** SFA25
8. Analyze and solve pairs of simultaneous linear equations.	
a. Understand that solutions to a system of two linear equations in two variables correspond to points of intersection of their graphs, because points of intersection satisfy both equations simultaneously.	**Lessons:** L89, LA92, LA93, LA94, LA97, LA99, LA100, LA102, LA104 **Other:** SFA18
b. Solve systems of two linear equations in two variables algebraically, and estimate solutions by graphing the equations. Solve simple cases by inspection.	**Lessons:** LA91, LA93, A94, LA99, LA100, LA102, LA103, LA104 **Other:** SFA18
c. Solve real-world and mathematical problems leading to two linear equations in two variables.	**Lessons:** LA92, LA93, LA94, LA97

Functions 8.F

Define, evaluate, and compare functions.

1. Understand that a function is a rule that assigns to each input exactly one output. The graph of a function is the set of ordered pairs consisting of an input and the corresponding output.[1]	**Power Up:** PS18, PU40, PU48 **Lessons:** L41, WP41, WP42, WP43, WP44, WP45, WP46, L47, WP47, WP48, WP49, WP50, WP51, WP53, L98, WP98, WP103, Inv11, LA98 **Other:** GC9, GC22, SFA21
2. Compare properties of two functions each represented in a different way (algebraically, graphically, numerically in tables, or by verbal descriptions).	**Lessons:** *L41, WP41, WP42, WP44, WP45, WP46, WP47, WP48, WP49, WP50, L88, WP98, Inv11* **Other:** SFA26
3. Interpret the equation $y = mx + b$ as defining a linear function, whose graph is a straight line; give examples of functions that are not linear.	**Lessons:** L56, WP56, WP57, WP58, WP61, WP62, L69, WP71, WP72, WP75, WP77, Inv11 **Other:** GC13, GC17, SFA22

Use functions to model relationships between quantities.

4. Construct a function to model a linear relationship between two quantities. Determine the rate of change and initial value of the function from a description of a relationship or from two (x, y) values, including reading these from a table or from a graph. Interpret the rate of change and initial value of a linear function in terms of the situation it models, and in terms of its graph or a table of values.	**Lessons:** L41, L44, WP44, L47, WP50, L69, WP69, WP70, WP77, WP95, WP100, LA68, LA98 **Other:** GC9, GC13, SFA27
5. Describe qualitatively the functional relationship between two quantities by analyzing a graph (e.g., where the function is increasing or decreasing, linear or nonlinear). Sketch a graph that exhibits the qualitative features of a function that has been described verbally.	**Lessons:** L41, WP41, WP42, WP43, WP44, WP47, WP48, WP49, WP50, L69, WP71, WP72, L88, Inv11, LA98 **Other:** GC13, SFA17

[1] Function notation is not required in Grade 8.

Key: **Inv:** Investigation   **PS:** Problem Solving   **SFA:** Standards Focus Activity
          L: Lesson   **PU:** Power Up   **WP:** Written Practice

Geometry 8.G

Understand congruence and similarity using physical models, transparencies, or geometry software.

1. Verify experimentally the properties of rotations, reflections, and translations:	
a. Lines are taken to lines, and line segments to line segments of the same length.	**Power Up:** PS22, PS84 **Lessons:** L26, WP27, WP29, Inv5, WP51, WP58, WP59, WP68, WP71, WP76, WP79, WP81, WP83, WP85 **Other:** GC10
b. Angles are taken to angles of the same measure.	**Power Up:** PS22, PS84 **Lessons:** L26, WP27, Inv5, WP51, WP58, WP59, WP68, WP72, WP76, WP79, WP81, WP84, WP85 **Other:** SFA3
c. Parallel lines are taken to parallel lines.	**Power Up:** PS22, PS84 **Lessons:** L26, WP29, WP51, WP58, WP59, WP76, WP81 **Other:** GC10, SFA3
2. Understand that a two-dimensional figure is congruent to another if the second can be obtained from the first by a sequence of rotations, reflections, and translations; given two congruent figures, describe a sequence that exhibits the congruence between them.	**Lessons:** L19, L26, Inv5, WP51, WP58, WP59, WP68, WP76, WP79, WP83, WP85 **Other:** SFA8
3. Describe the effect of dilations, translations, rotations, and reflections on two-dimensional figures using coordinates.	**Lessons:** L26, Inv5, WP51, WP56, WP58, WP60, WP68, L71, WP76, WP79, WP81, WP93, WP114 **Other:** GC10
4. Understand that a two-dimensional figure is similar to another if the second can be obtained from the first by a sequence of rotations, reflections, translations, and dilations; given two similar two-dimensional figures, describe a sequence that exhibits the similarity between them.	**Lessons:** L19, L26, WP27, WP34, WP36, WP38, WP40, Inv5, WP56, WP60, L71, WP71, WP81, WP93, WP96 **Other:** SFA9
5. Use informal arguments to establish facts about the angle sum and exterior angle of triangles, about the angles created when parallel lines are cut by a transversal, and the angle-angle criterion for similarity of triangles.	**Power Up:** PU11, PU14, PU16, PU19, PU64, PU66, PS92 **Lessons:** L54, WP54, WP55, WP56, WP58, WP59, WP61, WP62, WP63, WP64, WP67, WP68 **Other:** SFA11, SFA14, SFA24

Understand and apply the Pythagorean Theorem.

6. Explain a proof of the Pythagorean Theorem and its converse.	**Lessons:** Inv12 **Other:** SFA5
7. Apply the Pythagorean Theorem to determine unknown side lengths in right triangles in real-world and mathematical problems in two and three dimensions.	**Lessons:** Inv2, WP21, WP28, WP32, L37, WP39, WP46, WP55, WP59, WP62, WP65, WP68, WP70, WP72, WP75, WP82, WP88, WP91, WP92, WP93, WP94, L95, WP97, WP99, WP103, WP108, WP110, WP111, WP112, WP115 **Other:** SFA20
8. Apply the Pythagorean Theorem to find the distance between two points in a coordinate system.	**Lessons:** L96, WP96, WP104, WP111, WP114, WP115, WP119 **Other:** SFA6

Solve real-world and mathematical problems involving volume of cylinders, cones, and spheres.

9. Know the formulas for the volumes of cones, cylinders, and spheres and use them to solve real-world and mathematical problems.	**Lessons:** L76, WP76, WP78, WP79, WP80, L86, WP87, WP96, L106, L107, L111, WP111, WP112, WP113

Statistics and Probability 8.SP

Investigate patterns of association in bivariate data.

1. Construct and interpret scatter plots for bivariate measurement data to investigate patterns of association between two quantities. Describe patterns such as clustering, outliers, positive or negative association, linear association, and nonlinear association.	**Lessons:** Inv8, WP97, WP101, L113 **Other:** GC16, SFA23
2. Know that straight lines are widely used to model relationships between two quantitative variables. For scatter plots that suggest a linear association, informally fit a straight line, and informally assess the model fit by judging the closeness of the data points to the line.	**Lessons:** Inv8, WP97, WP101, L113 **Other:** GC16, SFA16
3. Use the equation of a linear model to solve problems in the context of bivariate measurement data, interpreting the slope and intercept.	**Power Up:** PS56 **Lessons:** WP66, Inv8, WP90, L98, WP101, L113
4. Understand that patterns of association can also be seen in bivariate categorical data by displaying frequencies and relative frequencies in a two-way table. Construct and interpret a two-way table summarizing data on two categorical variables collected from the same subjects. Use relative frequencies calculated for rows or columns to describe possible association between the two variables.	**Lessons:** Inv6, WP66, Inv8 **Other:** SFA13

Key:

Inv: Investigation	**PS:** Problem Solving	**SFA:** Standards Focus Activity
L: Lesson	**PU:** Power Up	**WP:** Written Practice

Solving Problems with Integer Exponents

Math Focus Solve real world problems involving powers and roots.

Essential Question How do I know whether to use a power or a root to solve a problem?

Activity

Materials:

48 color cubes

Let one unit be the length of each side of a color cube.

1. Make a prism with a height of 3 units and a square base, using all 48 cubes. What is the length of each side of the base of the prism?

   _____

2. Make a cube which is 3 units on a side. What is the volume of the cube?

   _____

Conclude:

3. How could you find the length of each side of the base of a square prism with a volume V and height h, without using small cubes? Hint: $V = s^2h$.

   _____
   _____

4. How could you find the volume of a cube that is s units on a side, without using small cubes?

   _____
   _____

Example 1 **Cube or Cube Root?**

Todd is inventing a new sport. He needs a foam ball with a diameter of 6 inches. How many cubic inches of foam would it take to make the ball, to the nearest whole number?

The formula for the volume of a sphere is $V = \frac{4}{3}\pi r^3$. Since the diameter is 6 inches, the radius is 3 inches. Substitute 3 for r and use 3.14 for π.

$$V = \frac{4}{3}\pi r^3$$

$$V \approx \frac{4}{3}(3.14)(3)^3$$

$$V \approx 113.04$$

It will take about **113 cubic inches** of foam to make each ball.

Problem Solving

REAL WORLD

Maggie is designing a lamp to hold 1620 cubic centimeters of beads. She wants the lamp to be in the shape of a square prism which is 20 centimeters tall. How long should she make each side of the square base?

The formula for the volume of a square prism is $V = s^2h$. Substitute 1620 for V and 20 for h.

$$V = s^2h$$
$$1620 = s^2(20)$$
$$\frac{1620}{20} = \frac{s^2(20)}{20}$$
$$81 = s^2$$

Since $s^2 = 81$, take the square root of 81 to find s. Thus, $s = 9$.
Maggie should make each side of the square base **9 centimeters**.

Practice

a. Kinetic energy, K, can be found with the formula $K = 0.5mv^2$, where m is the mass of the object and v is its velocity or speed. How much kinetic energy is produced by an object with a mass of 120 kilograms moving at a velocity of 8 meters per second? _____

b. Tonya has 8000 cubic centimeters of clay to form into a cube for a decoration. What should be the length of each side of the cube? _____

c. A sand bag, in the shape of a sphere, has a radius of 9 centimeters. What is the volume of the bag? _____

d. Multiple Choice Zachary has 4 cube shaped planters to fill with soil. If each planter measures 11 inches along each edge, how many cubic inches of soil will it take to fill all the planters?
  A 121 in^3 **B** 484 in^3 **C** 1331 in^3 **D** 5324 in^3

e. Multiple Choice The diagram at the right shows a path through a garden. The approximate length of the path, p, can be found with the formula $p^2 = 8^2 + 10^2$. Which of the following measures is closest to the length of the path?
  A 10 m   **B** 12 m   **C** 13 m   **D** 18 m

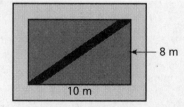

8 m

10 m

f. Reasoning In order to find the volume of a sphere with a radius of r, do you need to cube a number or find a cube root? Explain.

_____

_____

Estimate and Compare Irrational Numbers

Math Focus Estimate and compare irrational numbers.

Essential Question How can I estimate and compare irrational numbers?

Activity

Use the number line below to answer Exercises 2–6.

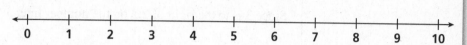

Irrational numbers cannot be expressed as a ratio of two integers. Their decimal expansions are nonending and nonrepeating. For example, $\sqrt{3}$ and π are irrational. In this activity you will estimate the square roots of irrational numbers using perfect squares and a number line.

1. Is $\sqrt{7}$ a rational number? _____

   Explain. _____

   _____

2. The number 7 is between which two consecutive perfect squares?

   _____ and _____, so _____ < 7 < _____

3. Take the square root of each perfect square, plot their square roots on the number line, and complete the statements below.

   $\sqrt{\rule{2cm}{0.4pt}}$ = _____ and $\sqrt{\rule{2cm}{0.4pt}}$ = _____

   $\sqrt{\rule{2cm}{0.4pt}}$ < $\sqrt{7}$ < $\sqrt{\rule{2cm}{0.4pt}}$

   _____ < $\sqrt{7}$ < _____

Hint

If the radicand is about halfway between the perfect squares, then use 0.5 for your estimate. If it is not, then estimate the tenths place based on the perfect square to which it is closer.

4. Find the *perfect square* to which 7 is closer.

   7 is closer to _____.

5. Since 7 is closer to the perfect square _____, then $\sqrt{7}$ is between 2._____ and _____.

6. Estimate $\sqrt{7}$ to the nearest tenth. _____

Name: _____

Example 1 Comparing Irrational Numbers

Replace each circle with the proper comparison symbol.

a. 3 ◯ $\sqrt{5}$

Estimate $\sqrt{5}$:　$4 < 5 < 9$
$\sqrt{4} < \sqrt{5} < \sqrt{9}$
$2 < \sqrt{5} < 3$

Since 5 is closer to 4 than 9, $\sqrt{5} \approx 2.2$.

Since 3 is to the right of 2.2 on the number line, **3 > $\sqrt{5}$**.

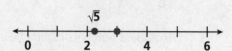

b. 4 ◯ $\sqrt{23}$

Estimate $\sqrt{23}$:　$16 < 23 < 25$
$\sqrt{16} < \sqrt{23} < \sqrt{25}$
$4 < \sqrt{23} < 5$

Since 23 is closer to 25 than 16, $\sqrt{23} \approx 4.8$.

Since 4 is to the left of 4.8 on the number line, **4 < $\sqrt{23}$**.

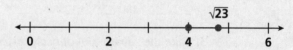

Practice

Estimate the irrational number. Then replace each circle with the proper comparison symbol.

a. $\sqrt{2} \approx$ _____,

$\sqrt{2}$ ◯ 2

b. $\sqrt{11} \approx$ _____,

3 ◯ $\sqrt{11}$

c. $\sqrt{10} \approx$ _____,

$\sqrt{10}$ ◯ 3

d. $\sqrt{6} \approx$ _____,

3 ◯ $\sqrt{6}$

e. $\sqrt{8} \approx$ _____,

2.5 ◯ $\sqrt{8}$

f. $\sqrt{3} \approx$ _____,

$\sqrt{3}$ ◯ 1.5

Properties of Transformations

Math Focus Explore the effects of transformations on angles and parallel lines in transformed figures.

Essential Question What properties of a figure are preserved under a transformation?

Activity

Materials:
Dynamic geometry software, pencil, protractor, tracing paper

Open a geometry application on either a hand-held device or on a computer. Then, either choose the polygon tool to draw a triangle, or chose the point tool and plot three points anywhere on the screen. Use the segment tool and connect the three points to form a triangle. Label the triangle *ABC*.

Use the point tool and plot a point outside the triangle. This point is the center of dilation. From this point, draw a ray through each vertex of the triangle. Point *D* is the center of dilation, and △*ABC* is called the *preimage*.

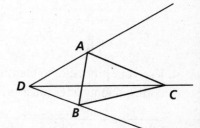

Select the transformation tool or the transformation mode in the application and chose *Dilation*. Enter 2 as the scale factor to dilate △*ABC* from the center of dilation. Label the vertices of the corresponding image *A′*, *B′*, and *C′*.

Use the angle measurement tool, and record the measures of the angles in the table.

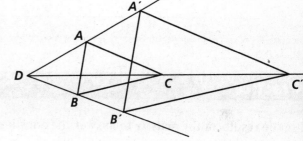

	Scale factor	$m\angle A$	$m\angle B$	$m\angle C$	$m\angle A'$	$m\angle B'$	$m\angle C'$
1.	2						
2.	0.5						

Math Language

Corresponding parts are sides or angles of congruent or similar figures that occupy the same relative positions.

Without changing the scale factor, drag the center of dilation or a vertex of △*ABC* to change the location of the image or the size and shape of △*ABC*. Delete △*A′B′C′* and dilate △*ABC* using a scale factor of 0.5. Record the measures of the angles in the table. Manipulate △*ABC* by dragging a vertex or dragging the center of dilation. Notice the relationship between corresponding angles.

$$m\angle A = m\angle A';\ m\angle B = m\angle B';\ \text{and}\ m\angle C = m\angle C'$$

Activity *(cont.)*

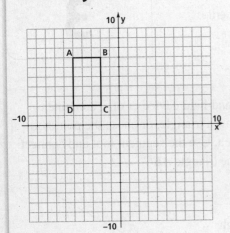

3. Trace the rectangle on a piece of tracing paper and cut it out.

Place your traced rectangle on top of the rectangle in the figure and translate it down 8 units and left 3 units. Draw the new location of the rectangle on the coordinate grid and label the vertices A´B´C´D´.

Use tracing paper to reflect the image of A´B´C´D´ across the y-axis. Draw the new location of the rectangle on the coordinate grid and label the vertices A´´B´´C´´D´´.

Use tracing paper to rotate the image of A´´B´´C´´D´´ counterclockwise 90˚. Draw the new location of the rectangle on the coordinate grid and label the vertices A´´´B´´´C´´´D´´´.

4. Use your protractor to measure the angles in the original figure. What do you notice about the corresponding angle measures in each image?

_____

5. In the original figure which sides are parallel? What do you notice about the corresponding segments in each image?

_____

_____

Practice

Use the results of the activity to answer the questions about angles and parallel lines in transformations.

a. Conclude. How do the measurements of the corresponding angles in the preimage and image compare in a transformation? Explain.

_____

_____

b. Conclude. What properties of a figure are preserved under a dilation, translation, reflection, and rotation?

_____

_____

c. Reasoning Why is the dilation of a figure called a similarity transformation? Explain using what you discovered in this activity and Lesson 26.

_____

_____

_____

_____

6

Name: _____

Using Irrational Numbers

Math Focus Solve real-world problems using irrational numbers.

Essential Question When would I use irrational numbers to solve real-world problems?

Activity

Materials:
protractor, compass, ruler, calculator

Hint

Pythagoren Theorem: In right △ABC, with a and b the lengths of the legs, and c the length of the hypotenuse, $a^2 + b^2 = c^2$.

Plot point A on a sheet of unlined paper and draw a ray at least 3 inches long. Label the ray $\overrightarrow{AB}$. Use a protractor and draw a ray perpendicular to $\overrightarrow{AB}$ at A. Set the width of the compass to 3 inches. Using A as the center of a circle, draw an arc intersecting the two rays. Label the points of intersection between the arc and the two rays P and Q. Draw $\overline{PQ}$ to create △APQ.

1. What kind of triangle is △APQ? _____

2. Use your ruler and measure PQ. _____ inches

3. Use leg lengths of 3 inches and the Pythagorean Theorem to calculate PQ.

What is PQ in radical form? _____ inches

4. Use a calculator to approximate your answer to Exercise 3 to the nearest hundredth. _____ inches

Conclude: Looking at your answers above, complete the statement.

5. If the legs in an isosceles right triangle have integer lengths, what is always true about the length of the hypotenuse? _____
_____

Hint

An irrational number cannot be expressed as $\frac{p}{q}$, where p and q are integers and $q \neq 0$.

Example 1 **Applying the Pythagorean Theorem**

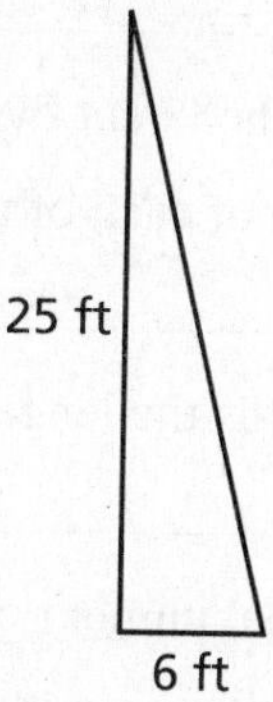

The top of a ladder, leaning against a building, is 25 feet above the ground. The bottom of the ladder is 6 feet from the base of the building. What is the length of the ladder?

25 ft

6 ft

a. If c represents the length of the hypotenuse in this triangle, what is c in radical form?

$$c^2 = 25^2 + 6^2$$
$$c^2 = 625 + 36$$
$$c^2 = 661$$
$$c = \sqrt{661}$$

b. What is c to the nearest tenth?
$\sqrt{661} \approx 25.7$
The ladder is **about 25.7 feet** tall.

Name: _____

Example 2   Using Heron's formula for the Area of a Triangle

History

Heron (Hero) was a Greek engineer and mathematician who lived in Alexandria about 1000 years ago. His formula for finding the area of a triangle with sides a, b, and c is

$A = \sqrt{s(s-a)(s-b)(s-c)}$

$s = \dfrac{a+b+c}{2}$

A small triangular garden has sides of 8 feet, 5 feet, and 11 feet. What is its area to the nearest tenth of a foot?

Use Heron's formula for finding A, the area of the triangle.

$$s = \frac{5 + 11 + 8}{2} = \frac{24}{2} = 12$$

$$A = \sqrt{12(12 - 5)(12 - 11)(12 - 8)}$$

$$= \sqrt{336}$$

$$\approx 18.3$$

The area of the garden is **approximately 18.3 square feet.**

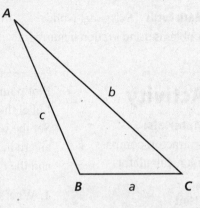

Practice

a. The dimensions of a rectangular door frame are 8 ft by 10 ft. A brace extends from one corner of the frame to the opposite corner. How long is the brace to the nearest foot?

_____

b. A 15-foot ladder is leaning against a building on level ground. The foot of the ladder is 4 feet from the base of the building. To the nearest foot, about how high up on the building is the top of the ladder? _____

c. The lengths of the sides of a triangular tile are 10 cm, 12 cm, and 20 cm. What is the area of the tile to the nearest square centimeter? _____

d. The formula for the area A of a square is $A = s^2$. The base of the Great Pyramid in Giza is a square whose area is nearly 53,000 square meters. What is the length of each of the sides of the base of the pyramid to the nearest meter? _____

e. The area of a square picture frame is 127 square inches. What is the length of the side of the frame to the nearest tenth of an inch? _____

f. The ratio of the sides of a rectangular TV screen is an irrational number called the *golden ratio*. Its value is $\frac{1 + \sqrt{5}}{2}$. What is the golden ratio to the nearest thousandth?

_____

g. Reasoning Use the definition of an irrational number and explain why the golden ratio is an irrational number.

_____

_____

The Pythagorean Theorem and Its Converse

Math Focus Explain a proof of the Pythagorean Theorem and its converse.

Essential Question How can I prove the Pythagorean Theorem and its converse?

Activity

Materials:

centimeter ruler, tracing paper (or photocopies of figure below), scissors, string or straws

History

There are many proofs of the Pythagorean Theorem, including one written by James Garfield, who later became President of the United States.

The Pythagorean Theorem states that in a right triangle, the sum of the squares of the lengths of the legs equals the square of the length of the hypotenuse. Complete the activity to demonstrate that this theorem is true.

Trace the figure below. Cut out the squares along sides a and b and then cut them on the dashed lines. Rearrange the parts so that they exactly cover the largest square.

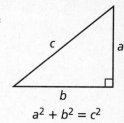

$$a^2 + b^2 = c^2$$

Write an expression in terms of a, b, and c for each of the following:

1. The area of the smallest square _____

2. The area of the middle-sized square _____

3. The area of the largest square _____

4. Conclude: $a^2 + b^2 =$ _____.

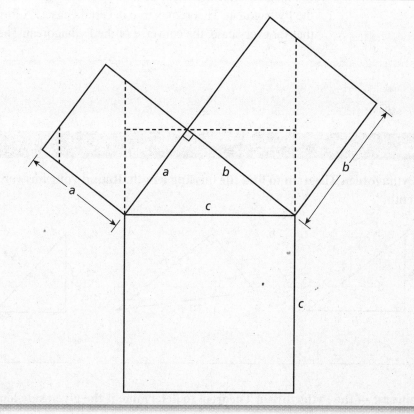

Name: _____

Activity (cont.)

The converse of the Pythagorean Theorem states that if a triangle has side lengths a, b, and c, and $a^2 + b^2 = c^2$, then the triangle is a right triangle. Determine whether the following side lengths make the equation $a^2 + b^2 = c^2$ true. Complete column four of the table.

	a	b	c	Is $a^2 + b^2 = c^2$ true?	Right Triangle?
5.	33	56	65	4225 = 4225, yes	
6.	36	77	85		
7.	39	80	89		
8.	48	55	73		
9.	65	72	97		

Measure lengths of straws 33 mm, 56 mm, and 65 mm. Cut the straws in lengths with these measures. Use the straw segments to form the sides of a right triangle. Repeat with the other side lengths. Record the results in column five of the table.

10. Based on the results recorded in the table, explain whether or not you think that the converse of the Pythagorean Theorem is true.

_____

_____

In this part of the activity, you have shown by observation that the converse of the Pythagorean Theorem is true in certain cases. A formal proof would show that for every case, the converse of the Pythagorean Theorem is true.

Practice

Use the Pythagorean Theorem to find the missing length. Round your answer to the nearest tenth.

a.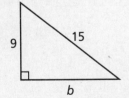

b.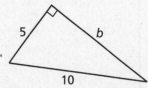

c.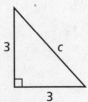

_____   _____   _____

Use the converse of the Pythagorean Theorem to determine if the given side lengths form a right triangle. Justify your answer.

d. 9, 40, 43   **e.** 12, 35, 37   **f.** 16, 63, 65

_____   _____   _____

The Pythagorean Theorem and Distance

Math Focus Find the distance between points in the coordinate plane using the Pythagorean Theorem.

Essential Question How can I analyze figures in the coordinate plane?

Activity

In coordinate geometry, you graph geometric figures in the coordinate plane. You can use the Pythagorean Theorem to find lengths of segments and analyze these figures.

$\overline{RS}$ has endpoints $R(2, -1)$ and $S(4, 3)$. In this activity you will find RS. (RS is the symbol for the length of $\overline{RS}$.)

Draw a horizontal segment through R and a vertical segment through S. Label the point of intersection T.

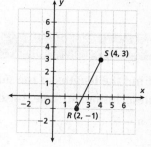

1. What kind of triangle is $\triangle RST$? _____

2. $RT =$ _____

3. $ST =$ _____

Use the Pythagorean Theorem to find RS.

4. $(RS)^2 = (RT)^2 + ($_____$)^2$

5. $(RS)^2 =$ _____$^2 +$ _____^{2} Substitute for RT and ST.

6. $RS = \sqrt{\rule{3cm}{0pt}}$ Take the square root of both sides.

7. $RS =$ _____   Use a calculator and round to the nearest hundredth.

Example 1 **Analyzing a Triangle**

Triangle ABC has vertices $A(1, 1)$, $B(7, 1)$, and $C(3, 5)$. Is $\triangle ABC$ isosceles, equilateral, or scalene?

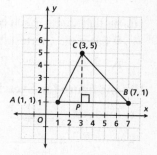

Find the lengths of the sides. Count squares to find AB: $AB = 6$.

To find AC and BC, draw a line from C perpendicular to $\overline{AB}$, and then use the Pythagorean Theorem.

$$(AP)^2 + (CP)^2 = (AC)^2 \qquad (BP)^2 + (CP)^2 = (BC)^2$$
$$2^2 + 4^2 = (AC)^2 \qquad\qquad 4^2 + 4^2 = (BC)^2$$
$$4 + 16 = (AC)^2 \qquad\qquad 16 + 16 = (BC)^2$$
$$20 = (AC)^2 \qquad\qquad\quad 32 = (BC)^2$$
$$4.47 \approx AC \qquad\qquad\quad 5.66 \approx BC$$

All three sides of $\triangle ABC$ are different lengths, therefore the triangle is **scalene**.

Name: _____

Problem Solving

A bee flies directly from point *X* to point *Y*. How far does the bee travel?

Use the Pythagorean Theorem twice, first to find *XQ*, and once more to find *XY*.

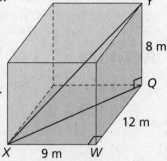

$9^2 + 12^2 = (XQ)^2$ △*XWQ* is a right triangle.

$81 + 144 = (XQ)^2$ Simplify.

$225 = (XQ)^2$

$15 = XQ$

$(XQ)^2 + (YQ)^2 = (XY)^2$ △*XQY* is a right triangle.

$15^2 + 8^2 = (XY)^2$ Substitute.

$225 + 64 = (XY)^2$ Simplify.

$289 = (XY)^2$

$17 = XY$ The bee travels **17 m.**

Practice

Find the lengths of the sides of the triangles. Then match each triangle with the best description: scalene, isosceles, or equilateral.

a.
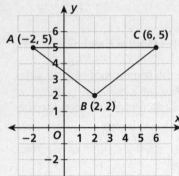

b.
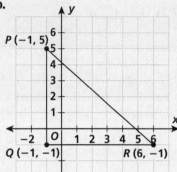

c.
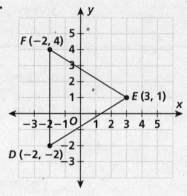

d. Multiple Choice Each edge of the cube shown is 4 cm long. What is the shortest distance from *A* to *G*?

   A $4\sqrt{2}$ cm   **B** 8 cm   **C** $4\sqrt{3}$ cm   **D** 12 cm

Use the figure for Exercises e–j.

e. Find *AB*. _____   **f.** Find *CD*. _____

g. Find *BC*. _____   **h.** Find *AD*. _____

i. Quadrilateral *ABCD* is either a _____ or a _____.

j. Reasoning How can you use the Pythagorean Theorem to prove which type of quadrilateral is in the figure?

_____

_____

_____

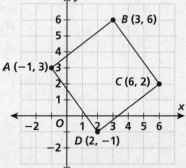

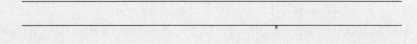

Solutions of Linear Equations: Special Cases

Math Focus Solve linear equations of the form $f(x) = g(x)$.

Essential Question What kinds of solutions will I find when solving a linear equation like $f(x) = g(x)$?

Activity

Materials:
Graph paper
Ruler

Hint

The symbol $f(x)$ represents the variable y in linear equations of the form $y = Ax + B$, where A and B are real numbers. This notation is used to indicate that the equation represents a function.

Linear equations such as $f(x) = 3x - 2$ and $g(x) = -4x + 5$ represent lines.

1. Complete the table below by finding the values of $f(x)$ and $g(x)$ for the given values of x.

x	$f(x) = 3x - 2$	$g(x) = -4x + 5$
0		
1		
2		

Now, on a sheet of graph paper, draw a set of axes. Label the horizontal axis x and the vertical axis y. Plot the points in the table and draw lines through each set of points.

2. What is the x-value of the point of intersection of the two lines? _____

3. What is the y-value of the point of intersection of the two lines? _____

4. Use the properties of equality to solve the equation $3x - 2 = -4x + 5$. What is the solution? _____

Conclude

5. What is the relationship between the solution of the equation $f(x) = g(x)$ and the graphs of the functions $f(x)$ and $g(x)$? _____

Example 1 **Verifying Solutions by Graphing**

Solve: $x + 5 = x + 10$. Verify your solution graphically.

Hint

You can use the Addition and Subtraction Properties of Equality to move a variable from one of side of an equation to the other in the same way that you can move numbers from one side of an equation to the other.

$$x + 5 = x + 10$$
$$x - x + 5 = x + 10 - x$$
$$5 = 10 \qquad ✗$$

Subtracting x from both sides of the equation results in a statement that is never true, $5 = 10$. Therefore there is **no solution** to the equation.

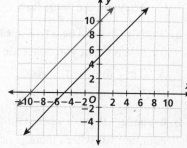

Verify the graphs of $f(x) = x + 5$ and $g(x) = x + 10$ do not intersect. The lines are parallel. This verifies the algebraic solution.

Name: _____

Example 2 Equations with an Infinite Number of Solutions

Solve: $2(x - 3) = 2x - 6$. Verify your solution graphically.

Distribute 2 on the left side of the equation and isolate x.

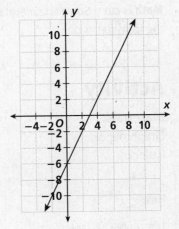

$$2(x - 3) = 2x - 6$$
$$2x - 6 = 2x - 6$$
$$2x - 6 - 2x = 2x - 6 - 2x$$
$$-6 = -6$$

The variable x disappears, leaving a true statement called an identity: $-6 = -6$. Therefore any value of x is a solution, and there are an **infinite number of solutions** for this equation.

Verify the graphs of $f(x) = 2(x - 3)$ and $g(x) = 2x - 6$ represent the same line. The two lines have all points the same.

Practice

Solve each equation.

a. $5x - 1 = 3x + 5$ _____

b. $9x + 2 = 5(x - 2)$ _____

c. $6x - 1 = 7x - x - 1$ _____

d. $-2x + 1 = 2(-x + 2)$ _____

e. Multiple Choice The solution of the linear equation $f(x) = g(x)$ results in an identity. What can you conclude about the lines represented by $f(x)$ and $g(x)$?

   A They intersect.

   B They are parallel.

   C They are the same line.

   D They do not exist.

f. Multiple Choice The solution of the linear equation $f(x) = g(x)$ results in a false statement. What can you conclude about the lines represented by $f(x)$ and $g(x)$?

   A They intersect.

   B They are parallel.

   C They are the same line.

   D They do not exist.

g. Multiple Choice The solution of the linear equation $f(x) = g(x)$ results in exactly one value for x. What can you conclude about the lines represented by $f(x)$ and $g(x)$?

   A They intersect.

   B They are parallel.

   C They are the same line.

   D They do not exist.

h. Reasoning Write a linear equation for which there is exactly one solution, a linear equation for which there is no solution, and a linear equation for which there are an infinite number of solutions.

_____

_____

Congruence Transformations

Math Focus Describe a sequence of transformations that maintains the congruence of the figures.

Essential Question How are transformations and figures that are congruent related?

Activity

Materials:
pencil, straightedge, thin paper or transparency film

Math Language

An image is a figure that results from a transformation.

Hint

The last transformation will need five prime marks since it will be the fifth transformation.

Hint

Use your thin paper to check the final image with the preimage or original figure.

Use thin paper or transparency film to help you draw the indicated transformations. Each transformation is applied to the image of the previous transformation.

1. Rotate triangle $\triangle ABC$ 90° about the origin.

   Translate the image down 4 units.

   Reflect the image across the y-axis.

   Translate the image right 6 units.

   Reflect the image across the x-axis.

   Label the final image with the letter of the applied transformation.

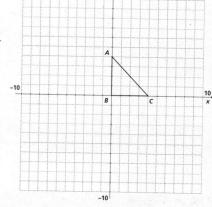

2. Compare the size and shape of the final image to the original triangle.

   _____

Congruent figures have the same size and shape. If two figures are congruent, then there is a series of rotations, translations, and reflections by which you can obtain one from the other.

3. Determine if the figures are congruent using your thin paper or transparency film.

   _____

4. Describe a series of transformations that will transform rectangle $ABCD$ into rectangle $A''B''C''D''$.

   _____

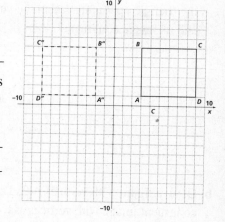

5. Reverse the order of the transformations. How is the outcome affected?

   _____

15

Activity (cont.)

Hint

These transformations will include a rotation.

6. Determine if the figures are congruent using your thin paper or transparency film.

_____

7. Describe a series of transformations that will transform trapezoid *CDEF* into trapezoid *C'D'E'F'*.

_____

_____

_____

_____

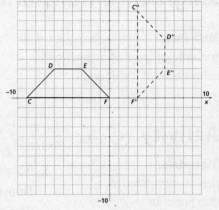

8. Reverse the order of the transformations. How is the outcome affected?

_____

_____

_____

Practice

a. Draw a triangle with vertices *A, B,* and *C* at (–7, –5), (–4, –2), and (–1, –5), respectively. Reflect the triangle over the *y*-axis. Then translate the triangle up 7 units. Label the vertices of the image. Are the triangle and its image congruent?

_____

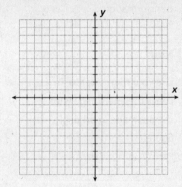

b. Draw a figure with vertices *A*(2, 1), *B*(5, 4), *C*(5, 5), and *D*(2, 5) and a congruent image with vertices (–1, –1), (–4, 2), (–5, 2), and (–5, –1). Label the vertices of the image. Describe a series of transformations that will transform the original figure to the second figure.

_____

_____

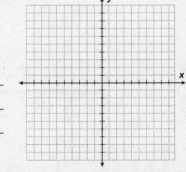

16

Similarity Transformations

Math Focus Describe a sequence of transformations that maintains the similarity of the figures.

Essential Question How are transformations and figures that are similar related?

Activity

Materials:

Pencil, protractor, thin paper or transparency film

Remember:

If two figures are similar,
- the corresponding angles have the same measure,
- the corresponding sides are in proportion.

A transformation that stretches or shrinks a figure is called a **dilation**. In a plane, the result of a dilation is a pair of similar figures. To create a dilation, the lengths of the sides of a figure are multiplied by a number called a **scale factor.**

The figure shows a dilation of $\triangle BCD$ that produces image $\triangle EFG$. The scaling factor was 3. Point A is the center of the dilation and segments through A pass through the pairs of corresponding vertices.

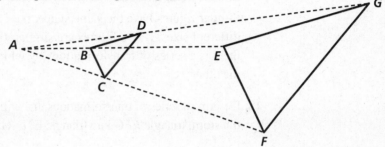

1. What are the three pairs of corresponding angles in the two triangles?

   _____

2. Use your protractor to measure each angle in $\triangle BCD$ and $\triangle EFG$.
   $m\angle B =$ ___ $m\angle C =$ ___ $m\angle D =$ ___ $m\angle E =$ ___ $m\angle F =$ ___ $m\angle G =$ ___

3. Are the measures of the angles changed in the dilation? Explain.

   _____

4. If $BC = 2$, $CD = 4$, and $BD = 3$, then what are EF, FG, and EG ?

   _____

5. What is $\frac{CD}{FG}$? Explain. _____

In the figure, $\triangle JKL$ has been dilated by a scale factor of $\frac{1}{4}$. Its image is $\triangle MNQ$.

6. If $JK = 32$, $LJ = 28$, and $KL = 44$, then what are MN, QM, and NQ? _____

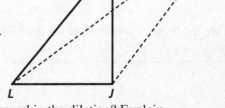

7. Use your protractor to measure each angle in $\triangle JKL$ and $\triangle MNQ$.
   $m\angle J =$ ___ $m\angle K =$ ___
   $m\angle L =$ ___ $m\angle M =$ ___
   $m\angle N =$ ___ $m\angle Q =$ ___

8. Are the measure of the angles changed in the dilation? Explain.

   _____

9. What conclusion can you draw regarding similar figures, their angle measures, and dilations?

   _____

Activity *(cont.)*

Hint

All dialtions are from the origin.

Apply the indicated transformations to the rectangle. Use thin paper or transparency film to help you draw the transformations. Each transformation is applied to the image of the previous transformation.

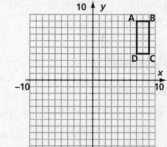

10. Translate the figure left 10 and down 2. Reflect the image over the *x*-axis. Enlarge the image by a factor of 2. Label the final image with the letter of the applied transformation.

11. Compare the size and shape of the final image to the original rectangle. Explain.

_____

_____

Similar figures have the same shape, but different sizes. If two figures are similar, then there is a series of transformations by which you can obtain one from the other.

12. Describe a series of transformations that will transform triangle *EFG* into triangle E‴F‴G‴.

_____

_____

_____

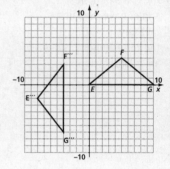

13. What do you know about the triangles in the transformations?

_____

Practice

a. Describe a series of transformations that will transform figure *ABCD* into figure *A‴B‴C‴D‴*.

_____

b. Are the figures congruent or similar? Explain.

_____

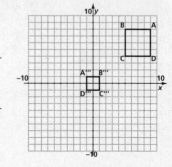

Add and Subtract in Scientific and Decimal Notation

Math Focus Add and subtract numbers expressed in scientific and decimal notation.

Essential Question How can I add and subtract numbers that are expressed in scientific and decimal notation?

Activity

In this exploration you will determine a rule for adding and subtracting numbers in scientific notation.

Decide if the following rule can be used to add numbers in scientific notation.

When adding numbers in scientific notation, write the addends with the same exponent of 10, and then add the coefficients and keep the base and exponent the same.

1. Write a sum with two numbers in scientific notation with the exponents of the base 10 being different.

_____ + _____

2. Rewrite the numbers so that both use the larger exponent value.

_____ + _____

3. Add the coefficients and keep the base and exponent the same.

_____ × 10⎯⎯⎯⎯⎯

4. Change the addends to standard form, add, and then rewrite the sum in scientific notation to check your answer. How do your answers compare?

_____

_____

Conclude:

5. Is the stated rule for adding numbers in scientific notation valid? _____

To subtract two numbers in scientific notation, follow the same rule for addition except subtract the coefficients.

Example 1 **Subtracting Numbers Written in Scientific Notation**

Subtract. Convert the answer to decimal notation. Which answer is more appropriate?

$(1.87 \times 10^5) - 460$

$(1.87 \times 10^5) - (0.0046 \times 10^5)$ Rewrite the second number using the larger exponent value.

1.8654×10^5 Subtract the coefficients. The base and exponent do not change.

186,540 **Since the number is not very large, the decimal notation is more appropriate.**

Example 2 Using a Calculator to Solve Problems in Scientific Notation

A CD is about 1.2×10^{-1} cm thick. A 12-inch vinyl record is about 1.9×10^{-1} cm thick. How much taller is a stack of 300 records than a stack of 300 CDs? Will 300 of each placed in two stacks on a shelf 4.5×10^{1} cm tall fit?

Enter $(300 \times 1.9E{-}1) - (300 \times 1.2E{-}1)$ on the calculator. The result is 21, so the stack of records is **21 cm taller** than the stack of CDs.

Enter $300 \times 1.2E{-}1$ on the calculator. The result is 36, so the CD stack is 36 cm tall.

Enter $300 \times 1.9E{-}1$ on the calculator. The result is 57, so the CD stack is 57 cm tall.

Enter $4.5E1$ on the calculator. The result is 45, so the shelf is 45 cm tall.

The stack of CDs will fit on the shelf. The stack of records will not.

Practice

Find the sum or difference.

a. $5.52 \times 10^{-10} + 6.19 \times 10^{-11}$ _____

b. $4.07 \times 10^{3} - 480$ _____

c. $6.3 \times 10^{7} + 9.3 \times 10^{9}$ _____

d. $1{,}580{,}000 - 6.31 \times 10^{3}$ _____

e. $2.6 \times 10^{8} - 590{,}000$ _____

f. $7.003 \times 10^{9} + 8.2 \times 10^{10}$ _____

g. $3.5 \times 10^{12} + 4.16 \times 10^{8}$ _____

h. $1.78 \times 10^{5} - 660$ _____

i. $3.44 \times 10^{6} - 69{,}800$ _____

j. $8.52 \times 10^{-13} + 4.23 \times 10^{-17}$ _____

Problem Solving REAL WORLD

k. The Moon is approximately 384,000 km from Earth. A star that is in line with Earth and the Moon is 1.97×10^{7} km from Earth. Use a calculator to determine the distance from the star to the Moon. Express your answer in standard notation and determine the most appropriate form for the answer.

_____

_____

_____

l. Reasoning When you add and subtract numbers written in scientific notation, how would the answer change if you used the smaller exponent for each number? Explain.

_____

_____

_____

Parallel Lines Cut by a Transversal: Angle Measures

Math Focus Explore properties of angles formed when a transversal intersects two parallel lines in a plane.

Essential Question What are the relationships and measures of angles formed when a line (transversal) intersects two parallel lines, segments, or rays?

Activity

Material:
Dynamic geometry software

Open a geometry application on either a hand-held device or on a computer. Then use the line tool and draw a line, labeling it $\overleftrightarrow{AB}$. Next, use the line drawing tool again and draw a line parallel to $\overleftrightarrow{AB}$. Label that line $\overleftrightarrow{CD}$. Now draw a third line, $\overleftrightarrow{EF}$, intersecting the two parallel lines. Mark and label the points of intersection between $\overleftrightarrow{EF}$ and the two parallel lines, G and H. Your labels should be placed as shown in the figure.

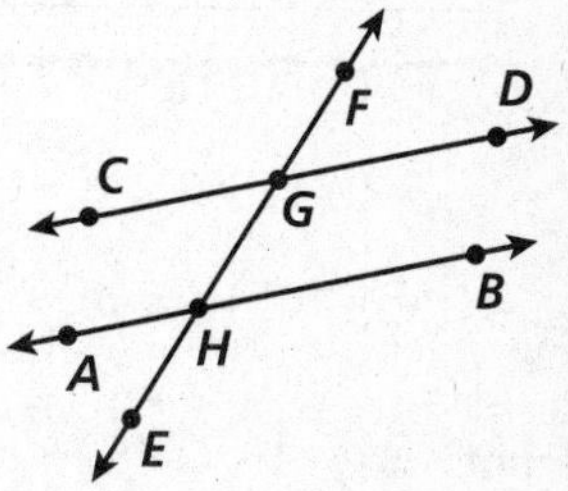

The angles formed by a transversal and a pair of parallel lines have special names depending on their locations.

- *Alternate interior angles* are pairs of angles that lie between the parallel lines and on either side of a transversal.
- *Corresponding angles* are pairs of angles that lie on the same side of a transversal, either both above, or both below, each parallel line.

Hint

In Euclidean geometry, two parallel lines in a plane do not intersect.

1. Name the interior angles in your figure. _____

2. Name the two pairs of alternate interior angles in your figure. _____

3. Name the four pairs of corresponding angles in your figure. _____

Now use the angle measurement tool and record the measures of the angles in your figure. Record these measures in the first row of the table below.

	$m\angle CGH$	$m\angle GHB$	$m\angle DGH$	$\angle GHA$
4.				
5.				
6.				

Next, rotate or drag $\overleftrightarrow{AB}$ and $\overleftrightarrow{CD}$ together in the plane. Alternately, drag $\overleftrightarrow{EF}$. After each manipulation, record the resulting measures of the four angles in the second row of the table. Drag the lines in this manner a third time. Again, record the measures of the angles in the third row of the table.

Conclude: Compare the angle measures noted in each row of the table. Then, answer the questions below.

7. When a transversal intersects parallel lines, what can you conclude about the measures of the alternate interior angles? _____

8. What conclusion can you draw about the measures of each pair of interior angles on the same side of the transversal? _____

Name: _____

Use the angle measurement tool and measure the corresponding angles in your figure. Record their measures in a table. Then drag or rotate the parallel lines or the transversal and measure the angles again. Repeat the manipulation a third time.

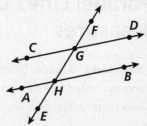

Conclude: Compare the angle measures noted in each row of your table. Then, answer the question below.

9. What conclusion can you draw about the measure of each pair of corresponding angles?

_____

From conclusions of the activities above, the following properties about the angles formed by parallel lines and a transversal can be used to find angle measures.

Hint	**Alternate Interior Angles**	**Corresponding Angles**
Congruent angles have the same measure.	If two parallel lines are cut by a transversal, then the alternate interior angles are congruent.	If two parallel lines are cut by a transversal, then the corresponding angles are congruent.

Practice

In the figure, lines *m* and *n* are parallel, line *t* is a transversal, and $m\angle 6 = 53°$. Use the figure to answer the questions below.

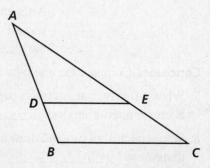

a. What angle corresponds to $\angle 6$? _____

b. What is $m\angle 4$? Explain. _____

c. What are two pairs of alternate interior angles? _____

d. What is $m\angle 1$? Explain. _____

e. What angle corresponds to $\angle 7$? _____

f. What interior angle is supplementary to $\angle 3$? _____

g. Reasoning In $\triangle ABC$, $\overline{DE}$ is parallel to $\overline{BC}$, $m\angle B = 112°$, and $m\angle C = 33°$. Complete the table below giving a brief reason for each angle measure.

Angle	Measure	Reason
$\angle ADE$		
$\angle AED$		
$\angle BDE$		
$\angle CED$		
$\angle A$		

Using Scientific Notation

Math Focus Solve real world problems using scientific notation.

Essential Question How can I solve a problem that uses numbers written in scientific notation?

History

The first recorded use of the term *scientific notation* was in 1961. The term became more widely used with the onset of computers and refers to a specific form of a number that includes a power of ten.

Rules for Numbers in Scientific Notation	
• Multiplication:	multiply the coefficients and add the exponents.
• Division:	divide the coefficients and subtract the exponent in the denominator from the exponent in the numerator.
• Addition or Subtraction:	rewrite all numbers so that they have the same exponents, then add or subtract the coefficients and the exponent stays the same.
• Rewrite:	rewrite any final answers that are not in scientific notation so the coefficient has one non-zero digit to the left of the decimal point.

Some areas of science require using measurements that are extremely large or extremely small. For example, the distance between objects in space is measured in light years. A light year is the distance light travels in a vacuum in one year.

One light year is approximately 5,880,000,000,000 miles, or 5.88×10^{12} miles in scientific notation. When solving problems that use light years, it is easier to change the numbers to scientific notation before performing an operation.

The map to the right shows the distances between certain stars. (ly = <u>light year</u>)

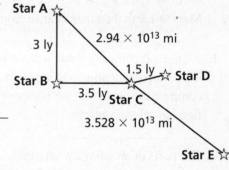

1. What is one way to find the distance in miles between Star A and Star B?

   _____

2. What is the distance in miles between Star A and Star B?

   _____

3. How many miles are between Star A and Star E? Explain your answer.

   _____

   _____

4. About how many times greater is the distance between Stars A and E than the distance between Stars A and B?

   _____

   _____

Example 1 | Solving a Real World Problem Using Scientific Notation

The parts of an atom are extremely small. About how many times greater is the mass of a neutron than the mass of an electron?

Mass of Parts of an Atom

Parts of an Atom	Mass
Neutron	1.67×10^{-27}
Electron	9.11×10^{-31}

Divide the mass of a neutron by the mass of an electron.

$$\frac{1.67 \times 10^{-27}}{9.11 \times 10^{-31}}$$

Divide the coefficient of the mass of a neutron by the coefficient of the mass of an electron.

$$\frac{1.67}{9.11} \approx 0.183$$

Subtract the exponent in the denominator from the exponent in the numerator.

$$\frac{10^{-27}}{10^{-31}} = 10^4 \quad \text{since } (-27) - (-31) = 4$$

The mass of a neutron is about **0.183×10^4 or about 1.83×10^3 times greater** than the mass of an electron.

Practice

a. The distance from Earth to the Moon is 3.84×10^5 km. The distance from Earth to Mars is 2.32×10^8 km. About how many times greater is the distance from Mars to Earth than the distance from the Moon to Earth?

_____

b. A large oil company made a profit of 1.564×10^{10} dollars during the first half of the year. The company continues to make the same profit for the rest of the year. Use scientific notation to compare the profit that the company will make by the end of the year to the profit made during the first half of the year.

_____

c. The parts of an atom are extremely small. A proton has a mass of 1.67×10^{-27}g. A neutron has a mass of 1.67×10^{-27}g and an electron has a mass of 9.11×10^{-31}g. Use scientific notation to compare the combined mass of a proton, neutron, and electron with the mass of an electron. _____

d. The Forget-me-not pollen grain is the smallest of pollen grains. It has a diameter of about 6×10^{-3}mm. A certain pollen mask can filter particles down to 3×10^{-4}mm. Use scientific notation to compare the diameter of the Forget-me-not to the particles that the mask can filter.

_____

e. Human hair ranges from 1.7×10^{-2}mm to 1.81×10^{-1}mm wide. How many times wider is the thicker hair than the thinner hair?

_____

     24

Two-Way Tables

Math Focus Understand data that is categorized in two ways.

Essential Question How can I construct and interpret the data in a two-way table?

Activity

Materials:
pencil, straightedge

Math Language

The frequency of an event is the number of times that the event occurs.

Hint

Use your straightedge to keep your place in the table. Align the straightedge vertically when you are working in a column. Align it horizontally when you are working in a row.

Data that is categorized in two ways can be displayed in a two-way table. The frequency of the data is displayed in columns to show one categorization and in rows to show the other categorization.

A poll of 300 moviegoers showed that 40% were male. It was found that 75% of the males liked the movie. Only 55% of the females like the movie.

	Liked	Disliked	Total
Males			
Females			
Total			

1. Enter the total number of moviegoers in the bottom right cell of the table.

2. Fill in the right column. 40% of the moviegoers were male. Find the total number of male moviegoers.

   40% of 300 = _____

3. Find the total number of moviegoers who were female.

   300 − _____ = _____

4. Fill in the top row. 75% of male moviegoers liked the movie. How many male moviegoers liked the movie?

   75% of _____ = _____

5. The remaining males disliked the movie. How many males disliked the movie?

   _____

6. Fill in the second row. 55% of female moviegoers liked the movie.

   55% of _____ = _____

7. The remaining females disliked the movie. How many females disliked the movie?

   _____

8. Fill in the last row. In each column, add the numbers in the first two rows to find the total number of male and female moviegoers who liked the movie.

You can check the accuracy of your table by checking to see that the totals in the first and second rows and the first and second columns are correct. Add across row one and then row two to check to check the column totals. Add down columns one and two to check the row totals.

Math Language

The relative frequency of an event is the ratio of the number of times that the event occurs to the total number of events.

Relative frequency can be used to determine if there is an association between the data values in a two-way table.

Example 1 **Interpreting a Two-Way Table**

A poll of 100 teens was conducted about whether or not they work after school and when they study. Use the table to determine if there is an association between working after school and studying in the evening.

	Work	Don't Work	Total
Study	15	45	60
Don't Study	30	10	40
Total	45	55	100

Find the relative frequency of studying in the evening:

Total who study in the evening = 60 $\frac{60}{100} = 60\%$
Total number of teens polled = 100

Find the relative frequency of studying in the evening among those teens who work:

Total who work and study in the evening = 15 $\frac{15}{45} = 33\frac{1}{3}\%$
Total who work = 45

Compare the relative frequencies: Teens who work after school are **less likely** to study in the evening than the general population of teens polled.

Yes, there is an association between working after school and studying in the evening. The relative frequency shows that teens who work after school are less likely to study in the evening than the other teens polled.

Practice

A poll of 200 male teens was conducted about whether they participated in a sport or played in the band. 45% of those polled participated in a sport. 60% of those males did not play in the band. 70% of the males who did not participate in sports did play in the band.

a. Construct a two-way table to represent the data.

b. Use the table to determine if there is an association between playing in the band and participating in a sport. Explain.

Angle-Angle Similarity

Math Focus Determine whether two triangles are similar.

Essential Question How can I show two triangles similar if two of their corresponding angles are congruent?

Activity

Materials:
notebook paper, protractor, ruler

Use a protractor and straightedge to draw $\triangle ABC$ and $\triangle DEF$ of different sizes so that $m\angle A = m\angle D$ and $m\angle B = m\angle E$. Use a ruler to measure the sides of the triangles. Then complete the table.

$m\angle A =$	$m\angle D =$	$AB =$	$DE =$	$\dfrac{AB}{DE} =$
$m\angle B =$	$m\angle E =$	$BC =$	$EF =$	$\dfrac{BC}{EF} =$
$m\angle C =$	$m\angle F =$	$AC =$	$DF =$	$\dfrac{AC}{DF} =$

1. What is true about corresponding angles of the triangles? _____

2. What is true about the ratios of corresponding sides? _____

3. **Generalize** What can you conclude about the triangles? _____

4. Draw a triangle on notebook paper using a protractor and ruler. Draw one angle that measures 40° and another that measures 55°.

5. Compare your triangle to the one drawn by your classmates. How are they alike? How do they differ?

_____

_____

Math Language

The Triangle Sum Theorem states that the sum of the measures of the angles in a triangle is 180°.

6. Find the measure of the third angle in your triangle using the Triangle Sum Theorem.

_____

_____

The results of the activity suggest that if two angles of one triangle are congruent to two angles of another triangle, then the triangles are similar. In addition to the definition of similar triangles, there are three ways to show that triangles are similar.

Proving Triangles Similar
Angle-Angle (AA) Similarity
If two angles of one triangle are congruent to two angles of another triangle, then the triangles are similar.
Side-Angle-Side (SAS) Similarity
If two sides of one triangle are proportional to two sides of another triangle, and if the included angles are congruent, then the triangles are similar.
Side-Side-Side (SSS) Similarity
If three pairs of sides of two triangles are proportional, then the triangles are similar.

Name: _____

Problem Solving

To find the width of the river, a surveyor drives stakes into the ground at points $P, Q, R,$ and S. He measures the distance between these points as shown in the figure. What is the width of the river?

$\angle PRQ \cong \angle TRS$ because they are vertical angles.

$\angle Q \cong \angle S$ because they both measure $90°$.

$\triangle PRQ$ is similar to $\triangle TRS$ by AA similarity, so corresponding side lengths are proportional. $\frac{QP}{ST} = \frac{RQ}{RS}$, so $\frac{20}{ST} = \frac{50}{75}$.
Cross-multiply to get $20(75) = ST(50)$; $ST = 30$.

The river is **30 m** wide.

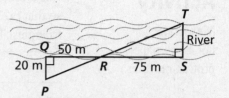

Practice

Determine if the triangles are similar. Justify your answer.

a.

b.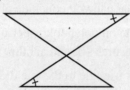

c.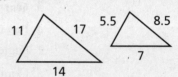

_____

_____

_____

d.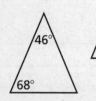

e.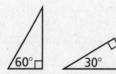

f.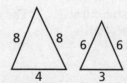

_____

_____

Problem Solving   REAL WORLD

g. A tree 10 ft tall casts a 12-ft shadow. Nearby is a telephone pole that casts an 18-ft shadow. If the triangles formed by the objects and their shadows are similar, explain why. If possible, find the height of the telephone pole.

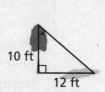 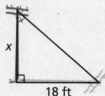

_____

_____

Proportional Relationships

Math Focus Understand proportional relationships.

Essential Question How can I find and interpret a rate of change?

Activity

Jamal decided to start saving $0.50 a day from his lunch money. The equation $y = 0.50x$ represents the situation, where x is the number of days Jamal has been saving and y is the total money he has saved.

1. Complete the table and draw a graph of the equation $y = 0.50x$.

x	y
0	
2	
4	
6	
10	

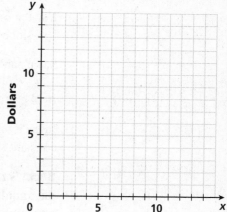

2. The y-intercept is the y-coordinate where the graph intersects the y-axis.

   What is the y-intercept of the line in the graph? $y =$ _____

3. What does the y-intercept mean in terms of Jamal's savings?

   _____

Math Language

Rate of change is a ratio of the amount of change in the output (y-values) to the amount of change in the input (x-values) variable.

4. What does the input variable represent? _____ What does the output variable represent? _____

5. Find the rate of change on day 2 (output/input). _____

   Find the rate of change on day 4. _____

   Find the rate of change on day 6. _____

Hint

Use $\frac{rise}{run}$ to find the slope of the line.

   Find the rate of change on day 10. _____

6. What do you notice about the rate of change in the variables? _____

   _____

7. Find the slope of the graph of the equation. How does it compare to the rate of change?

   _____

8. The output and input variables are in a proportional relationship. How can you describe a proportional relationship?

   _____

Name: _____

Example 1 Interpreting Slope and y-intercept

The table and graph show the number of games played compared to the number of points scored by Savannah and Becky, respectively. Find the rate of change in each relationship, determine if each relationship is proportional, and compare the rates of change in the two relationships.

Savannah's Scoring

Games	0	1	2	3
Points	0	6	12	18

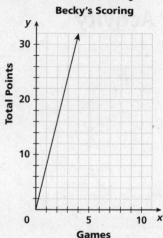

Becky's Scoring

Use the $\frac{output}{input}$ to find Savannah's rate of change. Use slope to find Becky's rate of change.

Savannah's rate of change : $\frac{6}{1} = \frac{12}{2} = \frac{18}{3} = 6$

Becky's rate of change: $\frac{16}{2} = 8$

In each relationship, the rates of change are constant so **each relationship is proportional**.

Becky's rate of change is higher than Savannah's, since she scored 8 points per game and Savannah scored 6 points per game.

Problem Solving

REAL WORLD

One day Jordan read 30 pages of a library book in 20 minutes. The next day he read 30 pages in 25 minutes. The third day he read 30 pages in 40 minutes. Is the relationship proportional? Justify your answer.

$\frac{output}{input}: \frac{30}{20} \neq \frac{30}{25} \neq \frac{30}{40}$

No. The ratios are not constant so the relationship between pages read and the time spent reading is not a proportional relationship.

Practice

Lani's Pace

Time (min)	0	2	4	6
Distance (ft)	0	200	400	600

Xena's Pace

Time (min)	0	2	4	6
Distance (ft)	0	300	600	900

a. Find the rate of change for the variables in each table.

Are the relationships proportional? Justify your answer.

Lani's rate of change: _____   Xena's rate of change: _____

_____

b. Compare the rates of change.

_____

Scatter Plots and Model Fit

Math Focus Fit a line to a scatter plot modeling a linear relationship between two sets of data.

Essential Question How can I draw a trend line to best fit a scatter plot showing a linear relationship?

Activity

Material:
grid paper, pencil, straightedge

Math Language

A trend line is also called a best-fit line and a line of best fit.

A trend line is used to make predictions about the data represented by a scatter plot that shows a linear relationship. The trend line models the relationship. A trend line is drawn so that the distance between each point on the scatter plot and the line is minimized.

A family collected data about the time and distance that they drove on a car trip over several days under varying weather and road conditions.

Car Trip

Time (hr)	0.5	1	1.5	2	2.5	3	3.5	4	5.25	6.5	7	8
Distance (mi)	25	68	60	133	125	215	210	278	341	390	406	520

1. Make a scatter plot of the data. Plot the points representing time in hours on the horizontal axis. Plot the points representing distance in miles on the vertical axis.

2. What type of relationship does the scatter plot show?

_____

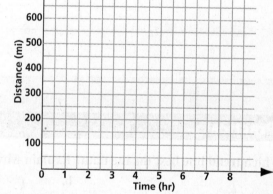

Car Trip

3. Draw a trend line using a straightedge. The trend line should have about the same number of points above it as below it.

4. Assess how well your trend line fits the data.

_____

_____

Hint

The interval on the y-axis is 50.

The interval on the x-axis is 0.5.

5. Use the trend line to predict the distance that the family could drive in 6 hours.

_____

6. Use your trend line to write an equation in slope-intercept form. Then use the equation to predict the distance that the family could drive in 6 hours.

_____

Activity (cont.)

The trend line used to model the data represented by a scatter plot can be used to make predictions. The more closely the line fits the scatter plot, the better the predictions that can be made using the line or an equation that models the line.

A 1-mile fun run will be held in 20 weeks. A novice runner preparing for the fun run recorded her best time every week over a 15-week period.

Week	Time (min)
1	30
2	35
3	29
4	34
5	29·
6	25
7	28
8	24
9	21
10	22
11	18
12	14
13	13
14	16
15	12

7. Use grid paper to make a scatter plot of the data. Label the horizontal axis "Number of Weeks". Label the vertical axis "Time (min)".

8. Describe the relationship between the number of weeks that the runner spent training and the number of minutes it takes the runner to run 1 mile.

_____

9. Draw a trend line.

10. Assess how well your trend line fits the data.

_____

11. Use your trend line to write an equation in slope-intercept form. Then use the equation to predict the time that the runner will take to complete the fun run on race day. Is your prediction reasonable?

_____

_____

Practice

Which trend line best fits the data? Explain why the trend lines do or do not fit the data well.

a.
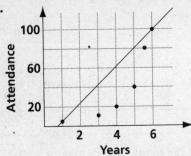

b.
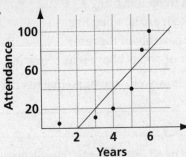

c.
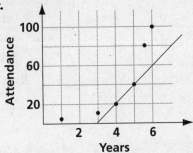

a. _____

b. _____

c. _____

32

Describe and Sketch Functions

Math Focus Draw and interpret qualitative graphs.

Essential Question How can I describe a functional relationship by analyzing a graph?

Activity

Materials:
Paper and pencil or pen

In this activity, you will examine how to draw a **qualitative graph**, one which does not rely on the details so much as on the general features of a situation. For example, as most people grow older, they get taller. One way to represent this would be with a simple graph.

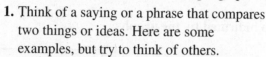

1. Think of a saying or a phrase that compares two things or ideas. Here are some examples, but try to think of others.

   "The bigger they are, the harder they fall."

   "Absence makes the heart grow fonder."

   "The more things change, the more they stay the same."

   "The more we spend on law enforcement, the less crime there will be."

   _____

2. Draw a qualitative graph showing how the two things in your phrase relate to each other. What assumptions have you made in drawing the graph?

   _____

   As shown above, sometimes you can illustrate a phrase with a graph. Now you will explore how to summarize a graph with words.

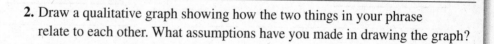

Interpreting data

Eight students were chosen at random. At the end of the school day, each one had his or her backpack weighed and grade point average (GPA) checked. The maximum GPA is 4.0. The results are shown in the graph to the left.

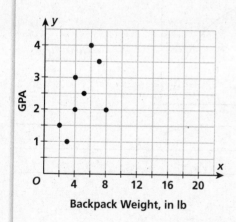
Backpack Weight, in lb

3. Draw a conclusion based on the graph that describes the relationship between the weight of the backpack and the GPA of the student.

   _____

   _____

4. Examine the individual points on the graph. Are there exceptions to the conclusion in Exercise 3? If so, discuss one of them.

   _____

   _____

5. For what conditions is the conclusion valid? For instance, does the conclusion hold if a student carries 50 lb?

   _____

   _____

Practice

Not all situations have graphs that are lines. Sketch a graph on notebook paper that shows the qualitative features of the function.

a. The population increased slowly at first, then it grew faster and faster over time.

b. The price of the company's stock remained constant for the first quarter, fell during the second quarter, then leveled off, and then rose during the final quarter to the price at the beginning of the year.

c. The smaller the capacity of the bus, the more buses will be needed for the field trip.

d. The number of people in the dining room is highest for lunch and less for dinner. Only a few people show up for breakfast. The dining room is closed between meals.

Describe a functional relationship indicated by the graphs.

e.
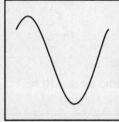

_____
_____
_____

f.
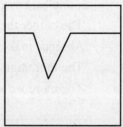

_____
_____
_____

g.
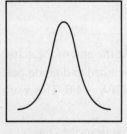

_____
_____
_____

h.

_____
_____
_____

Solving Systems of Linear Equations

ACTIVITY

18

Math Focus Understand the solutions of a system of linear equations.

Essential Question Does a system of equations have one solution, no solution, or infinitely many solutions?

Activity

Materials:
Grid paper, pencil, straightedge

Math Language

A system of two linear equations is two linear equations in the same variables.

Hint

When solving a system by graphing, use a straightedge to draw your lines.

The solutions to a system of equations are the points where the graph of the equations intersect.

Solve the system of equations: $\begin{cases} 3y - x = 9 \\ 2x = 6y + 12 \end{cases}$

1. Write each equation in slope-intercept form.

_____

_____

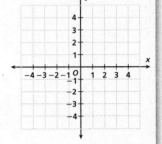

2. What do you observe about the equations? _____

_____

3. Graph each equation on the coordinate plane.

4. How many solutions does this system have? _____

Now solve another system of equations: $\begin{cases} x - 2y = 4 \\ 6y - 3x = -12 \end{cases}$

5. Write each equation in slope-intercept form.

_____

6. What do you observe about the equations? _____

_____

7. Graph each equation on the coordinate plane.

8. How many solutions does this system have? _____

9. Graph the system of equations on grid paper: $\begin{cases} 3x + y = 2 \\ x - y = 0 \end{cases}$

10. What is the approximate point of intersection of the system? _____

11. Isolate y in $x - y = 0$. _____

12. Now substitute the value you found for y in #11 for y in $3x + y = 2$.

_____

13. Solve the equation in #12 for x.   x = _____

14. Substitute the x value that you found in #13 for the y in either of the two original equations. Solve for the y value. Write the solution of the system as an ordered pair. How does your estimate compare to the exact solution?

(_____, _____) _____

Problem Solving

REAL WORLD

Two runways at an airport are parallel. If the equation $2x + 4y = 12$ represents one runway, which equation could represent the other runway?

A $x + 2y = 6$ **B** $2x = 12 - 4y$

C $y + 2x = 3$ **D** $2y = 12 - x$

Write the original equation in slope-intercept form.

$$2x + 4y = 12$$
$$4y = -2x + 12.$$
$$y = -\frac{1}{2}x + 3$$

Now write each line in (A) through (D) in slope-intercept form.

$x + 2y = 6$	$2x = 12 - 4y$	$y + 2x = 3$	$2y = 12 - x$
$2y = -x + 6$	$4y = -2x + 12$	$y = -2x + 3$	$2y = -x + 12$
$y = -\frac{1}{2}x + 3$	$y = -\frac{1}{2}x + 3$		$y = -\frac{1}{2}x + 6$

Only choice **D** represents a line with slope $-\frac{1}{2}$ and a y-intercept not equal to 3.

Practice

Graph to solve a–d. Does the system have exactly one solution, no solution, or an infinite number of solutions? If the system has exactly one solution, give the solution and check it algebraically.

a. $\begin{cases} y = 3x + 2 \\ y = 3x - 1 \end{cases}$ _____

b. $\begin{cases} y = \frac{1}{2}x + 2 \\ 2y = x + 4 \end{cases}$ _____

c. $\begin{cases} y + x = 3 \\ y - x = 3 \end{cases}$ _____

d. $\begin{cases} 2x + y = 1 \\ 5x - 2y = 1 \end{cases}$ _____

e. Multiple Choice The graph of which equation does not intersect the line shown on the graph?

A $y = -2x + 3$ **B** $y = -\frac{1}{2}x + 5$

C $y = 2x + 5$ **D** $y = \frac{1}{2}x + 5$

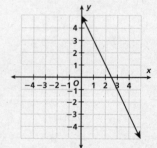

f. Multiple Choice What is the slope of a line parallel to $4x - 3y = 24$?

A -8 **B** $\frac{3}{4}$ **C** $\frac{4}{3}$ **D** 6

g. Solve by graphing:

$$\begin{cases} y = 2x \\ 3x + 2y = 21 \end{cases}$$

Check your solution algebraically. Show the check below.

_____

_____

_____

Using Square Roots and Cube Roots

Math Focus Use roots of perfect squares and perfect cubes to solve equations.

Essential Question How can I use square and cube roots to solve real world problems?

Activity

Materials:
64 color cubes

Make a large cube using all 64 of the color cubes. The volume of the large cube is 64 cubic units where a unit is the length of each side of a small cube.

1. What is the length of each side of the large cube?

_____

Make another large cube, this time with a volume of 27 cubic units.

2. What is the length of each side of the second large cube?

_____

Conclude: 3. How could you find the length of each side of a cube with a volume of V cubic units, without using small cubes?

_____

The solution of an equation $x^3 = a$ is $x = \sqrt[3]{a}$ where a is a real number. For example, if $x^3 = 8$, then $x = \sqrt[3]{8}$ or $x = 2$.

Example 1 Using Cube Roots

Carrie took a ride in a hot air balloon. The volume of air in the balloon was 288π cubic meters. Assume the balloon is in the shape of a sphere and use the formula $r^3 = \dfrac{3V}{4\pi}$ to find the radius of the balloon.

Substitute 288π for V and simplify.

$r^3 = \dfrac{(3V)}{(4\pi)}$

$r^3 = \dfrac{3(288\pi)}{(4\pi)}$

$r^3 = \dfrac{3(288)}{4}$

$r^3 = 216$

$r = \sqrt[3]{216}$

Think of perfect cubes: $4^3 = 64$, $5^3 = 125$, $6^3 = 216$.

So $\sqrt[3]{216} = 6$ and $r = 6$.

The radius of the hot air balloon is **6 meters**.

Name: _____

Problem Solving

REAL WORLD

The students at Skyline Middle School are designing a playground for the elementary school next door. They want the playground to be square and have an area of 144 square yards. How much fencing do they need in order to enclose the playground?

The formula for the area of a square is $A = s^2$.

$$144 = s^2$$
$$\sqrt{144} = s$$

Think of perfect squares or use a calculator to find that $s = 12$.

The playground will be 12 yards by 12 yards.

The amount of fencing is the perimeter of the playground.

$$P = 4s = 4(12) = 48$$

The students need **48 yards** of fencing.

Remember:

The solution to $x^2 = a$ can be positive or negative, but in word problems think about which answers make sense.

Practice

a. What is the radius of a beach ball that holds 972π cubic centimeters of air? Use the formula $r^3 = \dfrac{3V}{4\pi}$. _____

b. Multiple Choice Marcus has 512 boxes to stack in a the shape of a cube. How many boxes should he stack in the first layer?

A 4 boxes   **B** 8 boxes   **C** 16 boxes   **D** 64 boxes

c. Multiple Choice The formula for the period, T, of a pendulum is $T^2 = 4\pi^2 \left(\frac{L}{9.8}\right)$, where L is the length of the pendulum in meters and T is the time it takes to make one swing in seconds. If a pendulum is 39.2 meters long, what is its period, T?

A 4 seconds   **B** 8 seconds   **C** 4π seconds   **D** 8π seconds

Problem Solving

REAL WORLD

d. Katie is designing a cereal box in the shape of a cylinder, as shown in the diagram.

The formula $r^2 = \frac{V}{\pi h}$ gives the radius r of a cylinder with volume V and height h. What is the radius of the box Katie is designing? _____

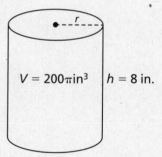

$V = 200\pi \text{in}^3$ $h = 8$ in.

e. Anna has 27 cubic feet of concrete to create the sculpture stand shown. What is the area of the base of the stand? _____

Solve each equation for x.

f. $x^2 = 169$ _____

g. $x^2 = 256$ _____

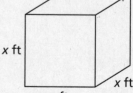

x ft x ft x ft

h. $x^3 = 125$ _____

i. $x^3 = 1000$ _____

Using the Pythagorean Theorem in 2-D and 3-D Figures

Math Focus Find unknown side lengths of right triangles in 2-D and 3-D figures.

Essential Question How can I use the Pythagorean Theorem to solve problems?

Activity

Materials: calculator, pencil, tracing paper

The relationship between the side lengths in a right triangle is used to find lengths in two- and three-dimensional figures. Recall that the sum of the squares of the lengths of the legs of a right triangle is equal to the square of the length of the hypotenuse.

Math Language

The legs of a right triangle form the right angle. The hypotenuse, always the longest side, is opposite the right angle.

1. Find the length of the hypotenuse without the use of a calculator.

$$a^2 + b^2 = c^2$$
$$4^2 + 5^2 = c^2$$
$$\underline{\hspace{1cm}} + \underline{\hspace{1cm}} = c^2$$
$$\underline{\hspace{1cm}} = c^2$$
$$\sqrt{\underline{\hspace{1cm}}} = c$$

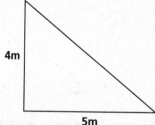

4m

5m

Math Language

The radicand is the number under the radical.

2. Find two perfect squares that the radicand is between.

$\sqrt{\underline{\hspace{0.5cm}}}$ is between $\sqrt{\underline{\hspace{0.5cm}}}$ and $\sqrt{\underline{\hspace{0.5cm}}}$. So, $\sqrt{\underline{\hspace{0.5cm}}}$ is about $\underline{\hspace{1cm}}$.
Check your answer with a calculator.

3. Use your tracing paper to trace the outline of the right triangle formed by the radius, height, and slant height of the cone.

Which part of the cone is the hypotenuse?

_____

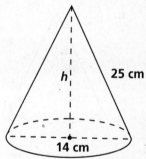

h   25 cm

14 cm

4. What is the radius of the cone? _____

5. Use the Pythagorean Theorem to find the height of the cone.

_____

_____

_____

_____

height of the cone = _____

Hint

The formula for the volume of a cone is $V = \frac{1}{3}\pi r^2 h$.

6. Use the height to find the volume of the cone. Leave the answer in terms of π.

_____

Name: _____

Example 1 Finding a Missing Length in a 3–D Figure

A garden sculpture is in the shape of a triangular prism with measurements as shown in the diagram. Estimate the height of the sculpture using the Pythagorean Theorem and then use a calculator to check the estimate. Will the sculpture fit under a tree without scraping against low-lying branches about 3 meters above the ground?

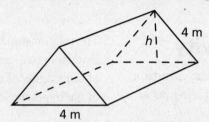

$$a^2 + b^2 = c^2$$
$$2^2 + h^2 = 4^2$$
$$4 + h^2 = 16$$
$$h^2 = 12$$
$$h = \sqrt{12}$$

Since 12 is between 9 and 16 and 12 is closer to 9 than 16, then $\sqrt{12} \approx 3.4$.

Estimated height ≈ 3.4 m   **Calculator check: height ≈ 3.5 m**

The sculpture **will not fit** under the tree without scraping against its branches.

Practice

Use the Pythagorean Theorem to find the missing length. Round your answer to the nearest tenth.

a.

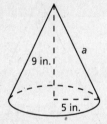

_____

b.

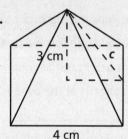

_____

c. A replacement brace had to be ordered for a shelf. The shipping container was 6 in. by 6 in. by 12 in. What is the greatest possible length of the diagonal, d, of the replacement brace?

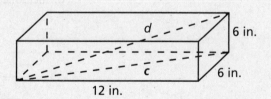

_____

d. You leave your house and walk 3 km due east and 4 km due south. How far are you from your house? _____

e. **Multiple Choice** What is the perimeter of the rectangle?

  A   8 cm   **B**   28 cm

  C   32 cm   **D**   48 cm

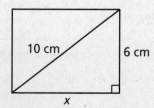

Applying Nonlinear Functions

Math Focus Describe volume as a nonlinear function.

Essential Question How can I describe the formula for volume as a function?

Rodney is designing a water tank in the shape of a cylinder that is 6 feet high. The radius of the tank can be between 2 and 5 feet.

Hint

The formula for the volume V of a cylinder with radius r and height h is $V = \pi r^2 h$.

1. Complete the table of ordered pairs to find the volume of the water tank for each radius. Round each volume to the nearest whole number. Use 3.14 for π.

Radius (r)	2	3	4	5
Volume (V)				

2. Use the points to graph the function $y = 6\pi x^2$ on the coordinate grid.

3. Does the graph appear to be linear or nonlinear? _____

Hint

A function is a rule that assigns to each input exactly one output.

4. How can you use the graph to verify that the relationship between the radius and volume of the cylinder is a function?

_____

_____

Example 1 **Solving Volume Problems with a Graph**

An aquarium needs to be 2 meters high, have a square base, and hold 12 cubic meters of water. The graph shows the relationship between the volume of a square prism with a height of 2 meters and the length of a side of the base.

Remember

If a vertical line can be drawn that passes through more than one point on the graph, then the graph does not represent a function.

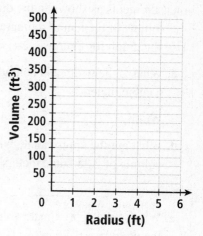

a. **What should be the length of each side of the base?**

When $y = 12$, $x \approx 2.4$. Each side of the base should be about 2.4 m.

b. **What is the volume of water the aquarium would hold if each side of the base is 1.5 meters?**

When $x = 1.5$, $y \approx 4.5$. The volume would be **about 4.5 cubic meters**.

c. **Is the relationship a function? Explain.**

Yes. The graph passes the vertical line test. Each input value has exactly one output value.

Practice

Is the function linear or nonlinear?

a. Volume of a sphere as a function of the radius: $V = \frac{4}{3}\pi r^3$. _____

b. Surface area of a prism with a length of 5 and width of 6, as a function of the height:

$y = 22x + 60.$ _____

Problem Solving REAL WORLD

A pup tent is in the shape of a triangular prism with
measurements as shown in the diagram. The graph shows
the volume of the tent as a function of the width, labeled as x.
Use the graph for Exercises c-e.

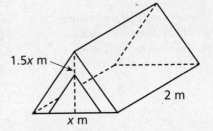

c. What is the width and height of the tent when it has a volume of
6 cubic meters?

Width = _____ Height = _____

d. What are the approximate width and height of the tent when it has a
volume of 2.25 cubic meters?

Width ≈ _____ Height ≈ _____

e. What is the approximate volume of the tent when
the width $x = 1.75$ m?

Volume ≈ _____

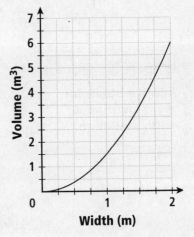

f. **Multiple Choice** Which of the following volume functions is linear?

A $V(x) = lwh$ when $l = x$, $w = 5$, and $h = 3$

B $V(x) = lwh$ when $l = x$, $w = x + 2$, and $h = 3$

C $V(x) = 0.5abh$ when $a = x$, $b = x - 3$, and $h = x + 1$

D $V(x) = 0.5abh$ when $a = 5$, $b = x$, and $h = x - 1$

g. **Reasoning** A rectangular prism has dimensions x, $x + 1$, and 2 inches.
The graph shows the relationship between the length x and the volume
of the prism. Explain how to find all three dimensions of a prism with a
volume of 12 cubic inches.

_____

_____

_____

_____

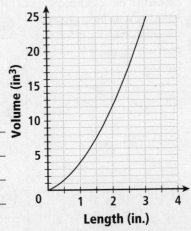

Linear and Nonlinear Functions

Math Focus Recognize an equation as a particular function.

Essential Question What can I learn about a function by examining its equation?

Activity

Materials:
graphing calculator

A function family is a set of functions whose graphs have similar characteristics. A function family can be formed through transformations of one function, called the parent function. The following chart shows the graphs of three parent functions.

Linear Function	Quadratic Function	Exponential Function

On a graphing calculator graph each equation. Name the parent function that correlates to the equation.

1. $y = 2x + 3$ _____

2. $y = x^2 + 1$ _____

3. $y = 3^x$ _____

4. $y = -2x + 2$ _____

5. $y = -x^2 + x + 1$ _____

6. $y = 0.25^x$ _____

Conclude: Describe the similarities of the x-term in each function type.

7. linear _____

_____

8. quadratic _____

_____

9. exponential _____

- The parent function of linear functions is $y = x$. The exponent of the x-term is 1. The graphs of all linear functions are non-vertical lines.
- The parent function of quadratic functions is $y = x^2$. The exponent of the x-term is 2. The graphs of all quadratic functions are parabolas.
- The parent function of exponential linear functions is $y = b^x$. The x-term is the exponent. The graphs of all exponential functions rise or fall on one end and approach a horizontal line on the other end.

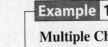 **Identifying a Function**

Multiple Choice Which equation could represent the graph shown at the left?

A $y = \frac{1}{2}x$ **B** $y = \frac{1}{2}x^2$ **C** $y = \left(\frac{1}{2}\right)^x$ **D** $y = x + 2$

The graph rises on the left side and approaches a horizontal line on the right side, so its equation is an exponential equation. The equation in choice C has the variable in the exponent, so it is an exponential function. The correct choice is **C**.

Problem Solving

REAL WORLD

The function $y = -8x^2 + 24x$ gives the height in feet of a soccer ball x seconds after it was kicked. Which curve models this function? Explain.

      A   **B**   **C**

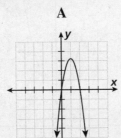   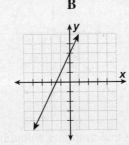   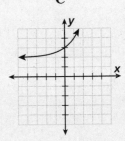

The function is a quadratic function so its graph is a parabola. The correct choice is **A**.

Practice

Match each function with its graph.

a. $y = 3x - 4$ _____

b. $y = 3x^2 - 4$ _____

c. $y = 3^x - 4$ _____

I. 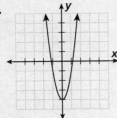   **II.** 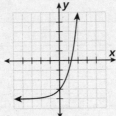   **III.**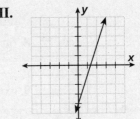

Identify the type of function the equation represents.

d. $y = 72 \cdot 6^{x-2}$ _____

e. $y = \frac{3}{2}(x + 4) =$ _____

f. $y = 3x^2 - 2x + 6$ _____

g. Reasoning Describe the difference between the linear parent function and the quadratic parent function in terms of their equations and their graphs.

_____

_____

SAXON MATH ACTIVITIES FOR COURSE 3   **44**

Patterns in Scatter Plots

Math Focus Determine patterns in scatter plots.

Essential Question How can I identify patterns in bivariate measurement data?

Activity

Materials:

grid paper, pencil

Bivariate data consists of two variables or data sets. The data can be graphed on a scatter plot and a relationship determined between the two variables.

Average Height of Girls in the U.S.

Age in Years	2	3	4	5	6	7	8	9	10	11	12
Height in Inches	33.5	37	40	42.5	45	48	50.5	52.5	54.5	56.75	59.5

1. Make a scatter plot of the data. Plot the points representing age in years on the horizontal axis. Plot the points representing height in inches on the vertical axis.

2. What relationship do you see in the data?

_____

_____

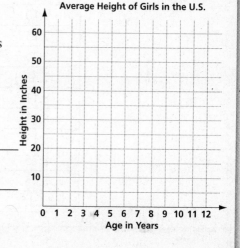

3. Do you think that this pattern will continue indefinitely as girls age?

_____

_____

Not all bivariate data have a linear relationship.

4. Describe the relationship between the number of purchases and the cost of an item as the cost increases.

_____

_____

5. Could a line be fitted to the points in the scatter plot? Explain.

_____

_____

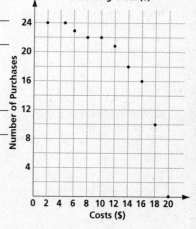

SAXON MATH ACTIVITIES FOR COURSE 3

Activity (cont.)

Math Language

A cluster is a set of closely grouped data.

Math Language

An outlier is a number in a data set that is distant from the other numbers in the set.

Some sets of bivariate data group, or cluster, around a point or line. Sometimes sets of bivariate data contain outliers that do not seem related to the data in the set.

Data was collected at a fast food restaurant to determine the times of day customers order breakfast. The table shows the number of customers served between 6 AM and 12 PM.

Number of Customers

Time (AM)	Number
6:00	9
6:08	9
6:14	10
6:22	11
7:00	8
7:10	9
7:15	9
7:20	7
7:35	8
8:11	10
8:15	10
8:18	11
8:25	10
8:45	9
11:15	1

6. Use grid paper to make a scatter plot of the data. Plot the points representing time on the horizontal axis. Plot the points representing the number of customers on the vertical axis. Label each axis.

7. Describe the relationship between the time of day and the number of customers ordering breakfast at the restaurant.

_____

_____

8. Explain why the data value plotted at 11:15 AM is an outlier.

_____

_____

Practice

Describe the relationship between the bivariate data as linear, nonlinear, or cluster. State if the data set contains an outlier.

a.
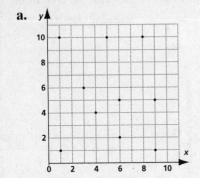

_____

b.
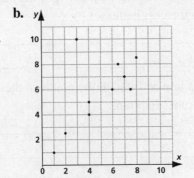

_____

c.
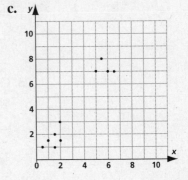

_____

46

Angle Relationships for a Triangle

Math Focus Relating the measures of the angles of a triangle.

Essential Question How can I use facts about the angles of a triangle to find the angle measures of a triangle?

Activity

Materials:
paper, pencil, protractor, scissors

The interior angles of triangles have a special relationship. In this activity you will use an informal argument to establish a fact about that relationship. An informal argument does not prove that every case is certain to have the same outcome. An informal argument does confirm its likelihood.

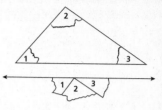

1. Draw a large triangle on notebook paper and cut it out. Label the interior angles 1, 2, and 3.

2. Tear off each of the three vertices of the triangle.

3. Plot a point on notebook paper and arrange the torn pieces around it so that all three vertices meet at the point with no overlap and no gaps between the torn pieces.

4. How do the pieces fit together around the point?

   _____

   _____

5. Use a protractor to measure the angle formed by the three torn pieces. What is its measure? What is the name of an angle with this measure?

   _____

   _____

Try this activity again using several types of triangles including acute, obtuse, and right.

6. What can you conclude from this activity about the sum of the measures of the interior angles of a triangle?

   _____

   _____

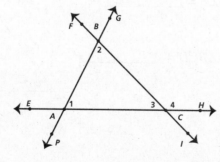

One side of a triangle and the extension of its adjacent side form an exterior angle. A triangle has six exterior angles, two at each vertex.

- ∠4 and ∠*GBC* are exterior angles

Each exterior angle has two remote interior angles. They are the interior angles that are not adjacent to the exterior angle.

- ∠2 and ∠3 are remote interior angles to ∠*EAB*

Activity (cont.)

A special relationship exists between an exterior angle of a triangle and its two remote interior angles.

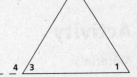

7. Draw a triangle and label the interior angles 1, 2, and 3. Extend one side and label the exterior angle 4.

8. What is the sum of the measure of the angles of the triangle?

   $m\angle 1 + m\angle 2 + m\angle 3 =$ _____

9. $m\angle 3 + m\angle 4 =$ _____ because they
   form a _____

10. Use **8** and **9** to complete this equation:

    $m\angle 1 + m\angle 2 + =$ _____ = _____ $+ m\angle 4$

11. The Subtraction Property of Equality can be used to show that:

    $m\angle 1 + m\angle 2 + =$ _____

    So, the measure of the exterior angle of a triangle is equal to the sum of its remote interior angles.

Practice

Use the given angle measures to find the measure of the indicated angle.

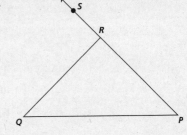

a. $m\angle P = 43°$; $m\angle Q = 55°$; $m\angle QRP =$ _____

b. $m\angle QRS = 134°$; $m\angle QRP =$ _____

c. $m\angle Q = m\angle P$; $m\angle QRS = 120°$; $m\angle Q =$ _____

d. $m\angle A =$ _____ e. $m\angle B =$ _____

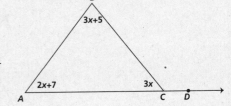

f. $m\angle C =$ _____ g. $m\angle BCD =$ _____

Solving Linear Equations

ACTIVITY

25

Math Focus Solve equations by collecting like terms and using the Distributive Property.

Essential Question How can I solve equations by collecting like terms and expanding expressions?

Activity

Materials:

A set of blue tiles containing six x tiles (x by 1 rectangles) and six 1 unit tiles (1 by 1 squares), a set of red tiles containing six $-x$ tiles (x by 1 rectangles) and six -1 unit tiles (1 by 1 squares), one paper bag

Blue algebra tiles represent positive terms and red tiles represent negative terms. Use the strategy shown below to organize randomly selected algebra tiles.

1. Place the blue tiles in the paper bag and randomly select 6 tiles. Group the like tiles together.

   Write the expression shown by the tiles._____

2. Add the red tiles to the bag and place the blue tiles back in the bag. Randomly select 6 tiles. Group the like tiles together.
   Write the expression shown by the tiles._____

3. What is the value of a set of matching red and blue tiles? _____

4. **True or false** Matching red and blue tiles can be removed to write an equivalent expression._____

Algebraic equations can be solved using the tile models.

Example 1 **Solving Algebraic Equations with Tiles**

Solve the equation $4x - 2 = 2x + 4$ using algebraic tiles.
Represent each side of the equation in tile form.

Now add or remove the same tiles from both sides with the goal of getting all rectangles on one side and all squares on the other side.

To get all rectangles on the left side, remove 2 x rectangles from each side.

To cancel the squares on the left side, add 2 1-unit squares to each side.

Now simplify the left side by removing all zero pairs.

Name: _____

> **Example 1** **(cont.) Solving Algebraic Equations with Tiles**
>
> Finally match up the rectangles and squares so that there is an equal number of squares (or portions of squares) for each rectangle.

> Each rectangle equals 3 squares so $x = 3$. Substitute $x = 3$ into the original equation to verify that the solution makes a true statement.

The Distributive Property can be used to expand an expression in an equation. Then like terms are collected, and the variable is isolated to solve the equation.

Math Language

When an algebraic expression is expanded using the Distributive Property, the parentheses are removed by multiplying each term in the parentheses by the number outside of the parentheses.

> **Example 2** **Using the Distributive Property to Solve Equations**
>
> Solve the equation $5(x - 7) + 4 = x + 1$.
>
> | Step: | Justification: |
> |---|---|
> | $5(x - 7) + 4 = x - 1$ | Given equation |
> | $5x - 35 + 4 = x - 1$ | Distribute |
> | $5x - 31 = x - 1$ | Combine like terms |
> | $4x - 31 = -1$ | Subtract x from both sides |
> | $4x = 30$ | Add 31 to both sides |
> | $x = 7\frac{1}{2}$ | Divide both sides by 4 |
>
> Check: $5(7\frac{1}{2} - 7) + 4 = 7\frac{1}{2} - 1$
>
> $\qquad 5\left(\frac{1}{2}\right) + 4 = 6\frac{1}{2}$
>
> $\qquad 2\frac{1}{2} + 4 = 6\frac{1}{2}$
>
> $\qquad 6\frac{1}{2} = 6\frac{1}{2}$

Practice

Use a tile model to solve the equation.

a. $6x + 3 = 2x - 5$ _____

b. $3 - 5x = 3x - 5$ _____

Solve each equation. Check your answer.

c. $2(x + 4) = 40 - 2x$ _____

d. $1 - (x + 1) = 8$ _____

e. $2(x - 3) = 3(x - 1)$ _____

f. $4(2x - 8) = \frac{1}{6}(36x + 54) + 7$ _____

Comparing Linear Functions

Math Focus Compare two functions represented differently.

Essential Question How can you find the slope using a table, graph, equation, or description?

Activity

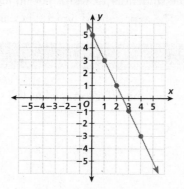

x	0	1	2	3	4
y	0	3	6	9	12

Hint

$$\text{slope} = \frac{(\text{change in } y)}{(\text{change in } x)}$$
$$= \frac{y_2 - y_1}{x_2 - x_1}$$

1. Find the slope of each function.

Graph: _____ Table: _____

2. Determine which graph has the steeper slope without graphing the function represented in the table.

_____

3. Write an equation for each function.

Graph: _____ Table: _____

4. Use the equations to tell which function has the steeper graph.

_____

Remember

For an equation $y = mx + b$, m represents the slope of the graph of the function.

5. Find the slope of each function.

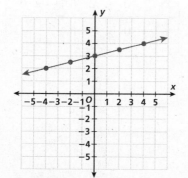

$$y = -0.5x + 3$$

Graph: _____ Equation: _____

6. Determine which graph has the steeper slope without graphing the function represented in the equation.

_____

7. Write an equation for the function that is graphed. _____

8. Use the equations to tell which function has the steeper graph. _____

Name: _____

An experienced typist can type 120 words in 2 minutes. The equation $y = 15x$ describes the rate of a typing student where x represents the number of minutes and y represents the number of words. Who types at the faster rate? Explain.

The rate of the experienced typist is $\frac{120}{2}$ words per minute or 60 words per minute. The rate of the student is 15 words per minute since the slope given in the equation is $\frac{15}{1}$. The experienced typist types at the faster rate.

Practice

a. Find the slope of each function. Determine which function's graph has the steeper slope.

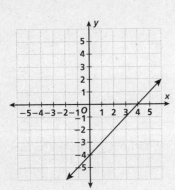

$$y = 8x - 3$$

Graph: _____ Equation: _____

_____

b. Find the slope of the function represented by the graph and the table. Which function's graph has the steeper slope? Explain.

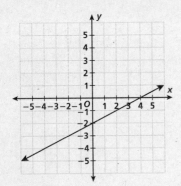

x	0	2	4	6	8
y	0	−1	−2	−3	−4

Graph: _____ Table: _____

_____

c. The charge for two hours of tutoring at Company A is $50. The equation $y = 20x + 5$ represents the amount charged by Company B, where x represents the number of hours and y represents the amount charged. Which company offers the better rate per hour? Explain.

_____

_____

Writing Equations to Model a Function

Math Focus Write the equation of a function.

Essential Question How can I find the slope and y-intercept given ordered pairs?

Activity

Materials:
40 counters, colored pencils, ruler

Place two counters in a stack. A second later, add three more counters to the stack. Continue creating a stack of counters at a rate of three counters per second. In the table below, record the total number of counters in the stack after each second.

1.

Seconds	0	1	2	3	4	5	6
Number of Counters	2						

2. Use any two ordered pairs from the table and the slope formula to find the slope of the line.

$m = \dfrac{y_2 - y_1}{x_2 - x_1}$ ordered pairs (_____, _____) and (_____, _____)

$m =$ _____

Hint

b represents the *y*-intercept of the equation of a line.

3. Use the value that you found for the slope and any ordered pair from the table to find the *y*-intercept *b*.

$y = mx + b$

(_____) = (_____)(_____) + b

$b =$ _____

Math Language

The slope-intercept form of the equation of a line is $y = mx + b$.

4. Write an equation that models the function

in slope-intercept form. _____

5. Choose two points from the graph.

(_____, _____) and (_____, _____).

6. Write an equation in slope-intercept form to model the function graphed.

Use the slope formula to find the slope.

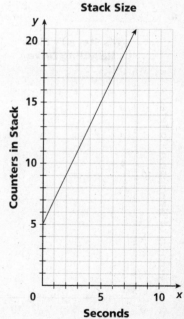

Stack Size

$m =$ _____

Use the graph to find the *y*-intercept. $b =$ _____

What does the *y*-intercept represent?

_____

Equation: _____

Name: _____

Problem Solving

REAL WORLD

Suppose that you took a canoe trip down a river at a constant rate. After 1 hour you are 5 miles from a nearby town. After 4 hours you are 11 miles from the town. Write an equation in slope-intercept form that models the function. Tell what the slope and y-intercept represent.

Slope: $m = \dfrac{\text{rise}}{\text{run}} = m = \dfrac{y_2 - y_1}{x_2 - x_1} = \dfrac{\text{number of miles}}{\text{number of hours}}$

Use $(1, 5)$ and $(4, 11)$ to find the slope: $\dfrac{(11-5)}{(4-1)} = \dfrac{6}{3} = 2$

The slope of 2 means that for every hour of the trip you have traveled 2 miles.

Find the y-intercept. Use $(1, 5)$ to substitute for x and y:

$y = mx + b$

$5 = (2)(1) + b$

$3 = b$

The y-intercept is $(0, 3)$ which means that at the start of the trip, the canoe is 3 miles from town.

The function is modeled by the equation $y = 2x + 3$.

Practice

Write an equation to model each function.

a. _____

Ms Steven's Class Recycling Drive

y-axis: Pounds of Newspaper Colleted

x-axis: Days

b. _____

Pedro's Quarter Collection

Number of Quarters	0	4	8	12	16
Value in Dollars	0	1	2	3	4

c. After 1 hour a family is 220 miles from their destination. After 3 hours they are 100 miles from their destination. Write an equation in slope-intercept form that models the function. Tell what the slope and y-intercept represent.

Deriving the Equation of a Line

Math Focus Use the slope formula to derive the equation of a line in slope-intercept form.

Essential Question How can I derive the equation of a line?

Activity

Hint

$$slope = \frac{(change\ in\ y)}{(change\ in\ x)}$$
$$= \frac{y_2 - y_1}{x_2 - x_1}$$

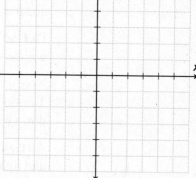

1. Plot a point at the origin and label the point $(0, 0)$. Plot another point anywhere in the first quadrant and label it (x, y). Draw a line through the points.

2. Substitute the points that you plotted into the slope formula and simplify the numerator and denominator.

   $m =$ _____

3. Multiply both sides of the equation by x. Give the resulting equation.

   _____

4. Write the equation with y on the left side. _____

   The equation in Problem 4 is the slope-intercept form of the line graphed in Problem 1. It is the equation of any line that passes through the origin. Now you will derive the equation of a line whose graph does not pass through the origin.

Hint

Recall that the y-intercept is represented with the letter b in the slope-intercept form of the equation of a line.

5. Give the coordinates of a point on the y-axis in terms of b. _____

6. Plot a point anywhere on the y-axis and label the point $(0, b)$. Plot another point anywhere in the first quadrant and label it (x, y). Draw a line through the points.

7. Substitute the points that you plotted into the slope formula and simplify the denominator.

   $m =$ _____

8. Multiply both sides of the equation by x. Write the resulting equation.

   _____

9. Add b to both sides of the equation. Write the resulting equation.

   _____

Remember

A vertical line is modeled by the equation $x = a$, where a is any real number.

10. Write the equation with y on the left side. _____

    The equation in Problem 10 is the slope-intercept form of the line graphed in Problem 6. It is the slope-intercept form of the equation of any line other than a vertical line.

Name: _____

Graph the function $y = 12 - 3x$, where x is the number of hours since Trisha started recording the temperature and y is the temperature she recorded.

Write the equation in the form $y = mx + b$: $y = -3x + 12$.

Identify the slope m and the y-intercept b: $m = -3$ and $b = 12$.

Plot the y-intercept at $(0, 12)$. From the y-intercept, use the slope to find another point on the line.

Note that the interval on the x- and y-axis is 2 units. The slope is $\frac{-3}{1}$. You can avoid estimating 3 units down by find an equivalent slope.

An equivalent slope is $\frac{-6}{2}$, since $\frac{-6}{2} = \frac{-3}{1}$. From the y-intercept count down 6 units and right 2 units. Plot the point.

Draw a line through the two points.

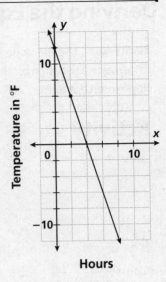

Practice

a. Write the equation of a line that passes through the points $(-2, 0)$ and $(4, 3)$. Graph the line.

Equation: _____

b. Write the equation of the line shown in the graph.

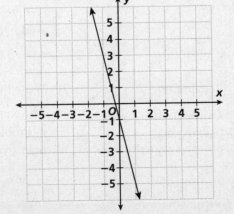

Equation: _____

Answers

Activity 1

1. 4 units
2. 27 cubic units
3. Sample: Divide V by h and then take the square root of the result.
4. Sample: Cube the side length, s to find the volume.

Practice

a. $3840 \text{ kg} \cdot \text{m}^2/\text{s}^2$
b. 20 cm
c. 3052.08 cubic centimeters
d. D
e. C
f. To find the volume of a sphere, use the formula $V = \frac{4}{3}\pi r^3$. So, you will need to cube the radius and multiply by $\frac{4}{3}\pi$.

Activity 2

1. No. Answers may vary. Sample: $\sqrt{7}$ cannot be expressed as the ratio of two integers, so it is irrational.
2. 4, 9, 4, 9
3. $\sqrt{4} = 2, \sqrt{9} = 3, \sqrt{4}, \sqrt{9}, 2, 3$
4. 9
5. 9, 2.5, 3
6. Answers may vary. Accept any reasonable answer. Sample: 2.6

Practice

a. Answers may vary. Accept any reasonable answer. Sample: 1.4, <
b. Answers may vary. Accept any reasonable answer. Sample: 3.3, <
c. Answers may vary. Accept any reasonable answer. Sample: 3.2, >
d. Answers may vary. Accept any reasonable answer. Sample: 2.4, >
e. Answers may vary. Accept any reasonable answer. Sample: 2.8, <
f. Answers may vary. Accept any reasonable answer. Sample: 1.7, >

Activity 3

1. Answers may vary. Sample: The angles should remain the same for any scale factor.
2. Answers may vary. Sample: The angles should remain the same for any scale factor.

3.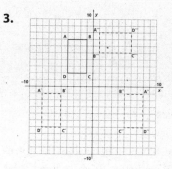

4. The corresponding angle measures are the same.
5. The corresponding segments that are parallel in the original figure are also parallel in each of the images.

Practice

a. Answers may vary. Sample: They are the same. A transformation does not change the angle measures.
b. Answers may vary. Sample: A transformation does not change the orientation of parallel sides in figures nor does it change the figure's angle measures.
c. Answers may vary. Sample: The dilation of a figure produces an image where the ratios between corresponding sides of the image and the preimage are equal to the scale factor and whose corresponding angles have the same measure. By definition, this means that under this type of transformation, the two figures are similar.

Activity 4

1. an isosceles right triangle
2. Answers may vary. Answer should be approximately: $4\frac{1}{4}$ in.
3. $\sqrt{18}$ or simplified, $3\sqrt{2}$
4. 4.24
5. The length of the hypotenuse will always be an irrational number. (Its length is $s\sqrt{2}$, where s is the length of each leg.)

Practice

a. 13 ft
b. 14 ft
c. 46 cm^2
d. 230 m
e. 11.3 in.
f. 1.618
g. Sample: The number $\frac{1+\sqrt{5}}{2}$ is irrational because the numerator $1+\sqrt{5}$ is not an integer.

Activity 5

1. a^2
2. b^2
3. c^2
4. c^2
5. yes
6. $7225 = 7225$, yes, yes
7. $7921 = 7921$, yes, yes
8. $5329, 5329$, yes, yes
9. $9409 = 9409$, yes, yes
10. Answers may vary. Sample: Since all of the given side lengths satisfy the Pythagorean Theorem, and they all made right triangles, then the converse of the Pythagorean Theorem must be true.

Practice

a. 12
b. 8.7
c. 4.2
d. no, $1681 \neq 1849$
e. yes, $1369 = 1369$
f. yes, $4225 = 4225$

Activity 6

1. right
2. 2
3. 4
4. ST
5. 2, 4
6. $\sqrt{20}$
7. 4.47

Practice

a. $AB = 5, BC = 5, AC = 8$; isosceles
b. $PQ = 6, QR = 7, PR \approx 9.22$; scalene
c. $DE \approx 5.83, EF \approx 5.83, DF = 6$: isosceles
d. C
e. 5
f. 5
g. 5
h. 5
i. rhombus, square
j. Sample: It's a rhombus because it has four equal-length sides. To show it is a square, find the lengths of the diagonals, and use the converse of the Pythagorean Theorem to show that every angle in the figure is a right angle.

Activity 7

1.

x	$f(x) = 3x - 2$	$g(x) = -4x + 5$
0	-2	5
1	1	1
2	4	-3

2. 1
3. 1
4. $x = 1$
5. Sample: The graphs of $f(x)$ and $g(x)$ intersect at the point whose x value is the solution to the equation $f(x) = g(x)$.

Practice

a. $x = 3$
b. $x = -3$
c. There are an infinite number of solutions.
d. There is no solution.
e. C
f. B
g. A
h. Samples: $3x + 4 = 2(x - 1)$, $3x + 4 = 3x - 1$, $3(4x - 1) = 12x - 3$

Activity 8

1.
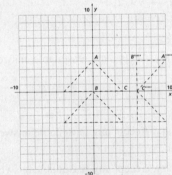

2. Answers will vary. Sample: They are the same.
3. Answers will vary. Sample: Yes. They are the same size and shape.
4. Reflect rectangle $ABCD$ across the x-axis. Then translate it 1 unit right.
5. Answers will vary. Sample: The outcome is the same. The order of the transformations doesn't matter.
6. Answers will vary. Sample: They are the same. They have the same size and shape.
7. Rotate trapezoid $CDEF$ 90° clockwise about the origin. Then translate it 3 units right.
8. Answers will vary. Sample: The outcome is the same. The figures are congruent.

Practice

a.

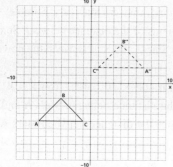

Yes, they are congruent.

b.

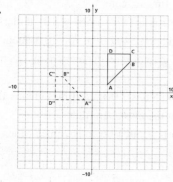

Rotate trapezoid ABCD counterclockwise 90°, then translate it down 3 units.

Activity 9

1. ∠B and ∠E, ∠C and ∠F, and ∠D and ∠G
2. Accept any reasonable answer. Sample:
   $m\angle B = 80°, m\angle C = 66°, m\angle D = 34°, m\angle E = 80°,$
   $m\angle F = 66°, m\angle G = 34°$
3. No. The two figures are similar, and in similar figures, the angles are congruent.
4. 6, 12, 9
5. $\frac{1}{3}$, △EFG is the enlarged image of △BCD. So the ratio of these two sides is the reciprocal of 3, the scaling factor.
6. 8, 7, 11
7. Accept any reasonable answer. Sample:
   $m\angle J = 90°, m\angle K = 40°, m\angle L = 50°, m\angle M = 90°,$
   $m\angle N = 40°, m\angle Q = 50°$
8. No. The two figures are similar, and in similar figures, the angles are congruent.
9. Answers may vary. Sample: The measures of corresponding angles are the same in a dilation. Two figures are similar if one can be obtained from the other with a dilation.

10.

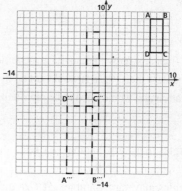

11. Answers may vary. Sample: The shape of the image is the same, but the size of the image changed. The figures are similar. The image of the original figure was obtained by a series of transformations.
12. Answers may vary. Sample: Rotate △EFG clockwise 90° around the origin. Reflect the image over the y-axis. Translate the figure left 4 units and up 3 units.
13. All of the triangles are congruent.

Practice

a. Answers may vary. Sample: Reflect the figure over the y-axis. Translate the image down 6 units and right 7 units. Contract the image by a scale factor of $\frac{1}{2}$.
b. Since the figure is contracted, the figures are similar. Their corresponding sides are proportional and their angles are congruent.

Activity 10

1. Answers will vary. Sample: 3.5×10^5; 2.6×10^2
2. Answers will vary. Sample: 3.5×10^5; 0.0026×10^5
3. 3.5026×10^5
4. Answers will vary. Sample: $3.5 \times 10^5 = 350{,}000$; $2.6 \times 10^2 = 260$; $350{,}000 + 260 = 350{,}260$; $350{,}260 = 3.5026 \times 10^5$. They are the same.
5. Yes

Practice

a. 6.139×10^{-10}
b. 3.59×10^3
c. 9.363×10^9
d. 1.57369×10^6
e. 2.5941×10^8
f. 8.9003×10^{10}
g. 3.500416×10^{12}
h. 1.7734×10^5

i. 3.3702×10^6

j. 8.520423×10^{-13}

k. $1.9316 \times 10^7 \, km$

l. Sample: The final answer would not have a coefficient of at least 1 but less than 10, so it would not be in scientific notation and would need to be rewritten.

Activity 11

1. Names of angles may vary. Sample: $\angle CGH$, $\angle GHA$, $\angle DGH$, and $\angle GHB$

2. Names of angles may vary. Sample: $\angle CGH$ and $\angle GHB$; $\angle DGH$ and $\angle GHA$

3. Names of angles may vary. Sample: $\angle FGD$ and $\angle GHB$; $\angle FGC$ and $\angle GHA$; $\angle DGH$ and $\angle BHE$; $\angle CGH$ and $\angle AHE$

4. Answers may vary. $m\angle CGH = m\angle GHB$; $m\angle DGH = m\angle GHA$

5. Answers may vary. $m\angle CGH = m\angle GHB$; $m\angle DGH = m\angle GHA$

6. Answers may vary. $m\angle CGH = m\angle GHB$; $m\angle DGH = m\angle GHA$

7. Alternate interior angles have the same measure.

8. Sample: Interior angles on the same side of the transversal are supplementary; i.e., the sum of their measures is $180°$.

9. Corresponding angles have the same measure.

Practice

a. $\angle 2$

b. $127°$; Sample: $\angle 2$ and $\angle 4$ are supplementary.

c. $\angle 3$ and $\angle 6$, $\angle 4$ and $\angle 5$

d. $127°$; Sample: $\angle 1$ and $\angle 3$ are supplementary.

e. $\angle 3$

f. $\angle 4$ and $\angle 5$; $\angle 3$ and $\angle 6$

g. Answers to reasons may vary. Samples given.

Angle	Measure	Reason
$\angle ADE$	$112°$	Corresponds to $\angle B$
$\angle AED$	$33°$	Corresponds to $\angle C$
$\angle BDE$	$68°$	Supplementary to $\angle B$ and $\angle ADE$
$\angle CED$	$147°$	Supplementary to $\angle C$ and $\angle AED$
$\angle A$	$35°$	The sum of the measures of the angles in a triangle is $180°$. That is, $m\angle A = 180° - (112° + 33°)$

Activity 12

1. Sample: Use the scientific notation for light year and multiply the coefficient (5.88) by 3.

2. 17.64×10^{12} miles or 1.764×10^{13} miles (in scientific notation) or 17,640,000,000,000 miles

3. 6.468×10^{13} miles; Answers may vary. Sample: Add the coefficients of the distance between Star A and Star C plus Star C and Star E. Keep the power of ten the same.

4. The quotient of 6.468×10^{13} and 1.764×10^{13} is about 3.7. So the distance between Stars A and E is about 3.7 times the distance between Stars A and B.

Practice

a. about 6.0×10^2 times greater

b. 3.128×10^{10} dollars is twice 1.564×10^{10} dollars

c. The combined mass 3.340911×10^{-27} g is about 3.7×10^3 times greater than the mass of an electron 9.11×10^{-31} g.

d. Forget-me-not pollen is 2.0×10^1 times greater than the particles that the mask can filter.

e. The thicker hair is about 1.06×10^1 times wider.

Activity 13

1. 300

2. 120

3. 120, 180

4. 120, 90

5. 30

6. 180, 99

7. 81

8.

	Liked	Disliked	Total
Males	90	30	120
Females	99	81	180
Total	189	111	300

Practice

a.

	Band	No Band	Total
Sports	36	54	90
No Sports	77	33	110
Total	113	87	200

b. $\frac{90}{200}$, or 45%, of all male teens polled participated in a sport. $\frac{36}{113}$, or about 32%, of male teens who played in the band also participated in a sport. Yes, there is an association between playing in the band and participating in a sport. The relative frequency shows that male teens who participate in a sport are less likely to play in the band than the general population of male teens polled.

Activity 14

Answers in table may vary. Check students' work

1. They have equal measures.
2. They are equal.
3. They are similar.
4.

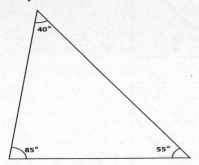

5. Answers will vary. Sample: The triangles have the same shape, but they are different sizes.
6. $180° - 40° - 55° = 85°$. The third angle measures 85°.

Practice

a. Yes, by AA similarity.
b. Yes, by AA similarity.
c. Yes, by SSS similarity.
d. No. There is only one pair of corresponding angles with the same measure.
e. Yes, by AA similarity.
f. Yes, by SSS similarity.
g. Answers may vary. Sample: Yes the triangles are similar by AA similarity. The telephone pole is 15 ft high.

Activity 15

1. 0, 1, 2, 3, 5;

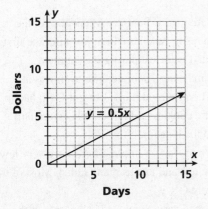

2. 0
3. Answer may vary. Sample: Jamal had $0 before he started saving money each day.
4. The input variable represents the number of days that Jamal has been saving. The output variable represents the total number of dollars saved.

5. Day 2: $\frac{1}{2}$, Day 4: $\frac{2}{4} = \frac{1}{2}$, Day 6: $\frac{3}{6} = \frac{1}{2}$, Day 10: $\frac{5}{10} = \frac{1}{2}$
6. Answers may vary. Sample: The rate of change is constant.
7. Slope: $\frac{1}{2}$, The slope of the graph and the rate of change are the same.
8. Answers may vary. Sample: In a proportional relationship the ratio between the output and input variables is the same, so the rate of change is constant.

Practice

a. Lani: $\frac{100}{1}$, Xena: $\frac{150}{1}$; Answers may vary. Sample: Each relationship is proportional because they both have a constant rate of change.
b. Xena's rate of change is greater than Lani's because she walks at pace of 150 ft/min. Lani walks at a pace of 100 ft/min.

Activity 16

1.

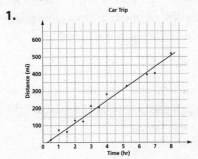

2. linear
3. Answers will vary. Sample: See answer to Activity 16 problem 1.
4. Answers will vary. Sample: All of the data points are close to the line so the trend line fits the data well.
5. Answers will vary. Sample: They could drive about 380 miles.
6. Answers will vary. Sample: $y = 65x$. Using the equation to predict the distance, the family could drive about 390 mi.
7.

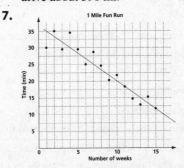

8. linear

9. Answers will vary. Sample: See answer to Activity 16 problem 7.

10. Answers will vary. Sample: Nearly all of the data points are close to the line so the trend line fits the data well.

11. Answers will vary. Sample: $y = -\frac{5}{3}x + 36$. The prediction using the equation is that it would take the runner about 2.7 min to complete the run. This prediction is not reasonable due to human limitations.

Practice

a. Answers will vary. Sample: Most of the data points fall below the trend line, so the line is not a good fit.

b. Answers will vary. Sample: Line of best fit. The data points are reasonably close to the line and there are an equal number of data points above and below the line.

c. Answers will vary. Sample: The line is drawn using two data values that are linear, but four other points are above the line. The line is not a good fit.

Activity 17

1. Answers will vary. Sample: The lower the outdoor temperature, the higher we set the thermostat.

2. Answers will vary. Sample:

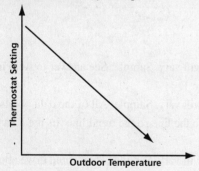

An assumption is that everyone sets the thermostat higher in cold weather.

3. As the weight of a student's backpack increases, the GPA increases.

4. Yes, there are exceptions. Sample: For example, the student with the heaviest backpack (8 lb) did not have the highest GPA.

5. Sample: The conclusion appears to be valid for those conditions represented on the graph—for backpacks no heavier than around 20 lb. It wouldn't follow that, if a student carried a 50 lb packpack, his or her GPA would be higher than 4.0, since there are no values for a GPA greater than 4.0

Practice

a.

b.

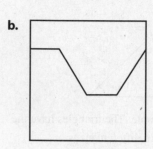

c.

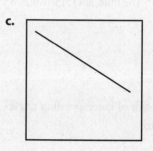

d.

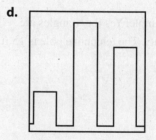

e. Answers may vary. Sample: Attendance at the mountain resort reaches a high just after the first of the year and is lowest during the summer.

f. Answers may vary. Sample: The oven was at 350° F. Then I turned it off. I forgot I still had to make more cookies so I turned it back on until it reached 350° F again.

g. Answers may vary. Sample: There were very few A's on the test and just as many failed. Most of the grades were C's.

h. Answers may vary. Sample: The volume of the block of ice began to decrease slowly as the ice melted. Then it decreased more rapidly until all of the ice was gone.

Activity 18

1. $y = \frac{1}{3}x + 3$, $y = \frac{1}{3}x - 2$
2. They have the same slope.
3.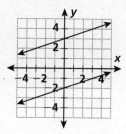

4. none
5. $y = \frac{1}{2}x - 2$, $y = \frac{1}{2}x - 2$
6. They are the same.
7.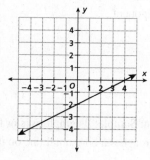

8. infinitely many
9.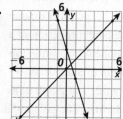

10. Answers will vary. Sample: $(\frac{1}{2}, \frac{1}{2})$
11. $y = x$
12. $3x + x = 2$
13. $x = \frac{1}{2}$
14. $(\frac{1}{2}, \frac{1}{2})$, Answers will vary. Sample: My estimate and the exact value are the same.

Practice

a. no solution

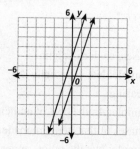

b. infinitely many solutions

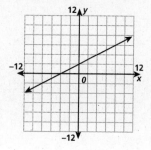

c. (0, 3)

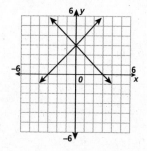

$y = 3 - x$, $3 - x - x = 3$, $-2x = 0$, $x = 0$
$y + x = 3$, $y + 0 = 3$, $y = 3$

d. $(\frac{1}{3}, \frac{1}{3})$

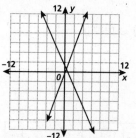

$y = 1 - 2x$, $5x - 2y = 1$, $5x - 2(1 - 2x) = 1$,
$9x = 3$, $x = \frac{1}{3}$, $y = 1 - 2(\frac{1}{3}) = \frac{1}{3}$

e. A
f. C
g. (3, 6)

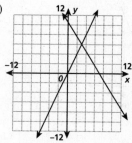

$y = 2x$, $3x + 2(2x) = 21$, $7x = 21$, $x = 3$ $y = 2x$,
$y = 2(3)$, $y = 6$

Activity 19

1. 4 units
2. 3 units
3. Answers may vary. Sample: Take the cube root of V.

Practice

a. 9 cm
b. D
c. C
d. 5 in.
e. 9 square feet
f. $x = \pm 13$
g. $x = \pm 16$
h. $x = 5$
i. $x = 10$

Activity 20

1. $16, 25, 41, \sqrt{41}$
2. $41, 36, 49, 41$, about 6.4 m
3. slant height
4. 7 cm
5. 24 cm
6. 392π cm

Practice

a. $a \approx 10.3$ in.
b. $c \approx 3.6$ cm
c. $c = \sqrt{180}$ in., $d \approx 14.7$ in.
d. 5 km
e. B

Activity 21

1.

Radius (r)	2	3	4	5
Volume (V)	75	170	302	471

2.

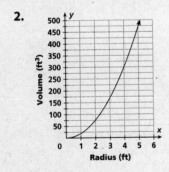

3. nonlinear
4. Answers may vary. Sample: The curve verifies that every r value has one and only one V value. The graph passes the vertical line test.

Practice

a. nonlinear
b. linear
c. 2 m; 3 m
d. 1.25 m; 1.88 m
e. 4.5 m³

f. A
g. Sample: In the graph, when $y = 12$, $x = 2$. When $x = 2$, $x + 1 = 3$. The dimensions are 2 in. by 3 in. by 2 in.

Activity 22

1. linear
2. quadratic
3. exponential
4. linear
5. quadratic
6. exponential
7. The x-term has an exponent of 1.
8. At least one x-term has an exponent of 2.
9. The x-term is the exponent.

Practice

a. III
b. I
c. II
d. exponential function; Sample: Its graph rises or falls on one end and approaches a horizontal line on the other end.
e. linear function; Sample: Its graph is a line.
f. quadratic function; Sample: Its graph is a parabola.
g. Sample: The x-term in the parent function of a linear equation has an exponent of 1 while the x-term in the parent function of a quadratic function has an exponent of 2. The graph of a linear function is a straight line. The graph of a quadratic function is a u-shaped parabola.

Activity 23

1.

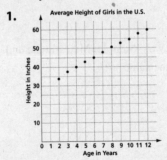

2. As age in years increases, so does height.
3. Answers will vary. Sample: No, eventually the heights will stop increasing.
4. Answers will vary. Sample: As the cost of an item increases, fewer purchases of that item are made.
5. Answers will vary. Sample: No, the points appear to curve down to the right and then drop off steeply. The points do not tend to cluster around line.

6.

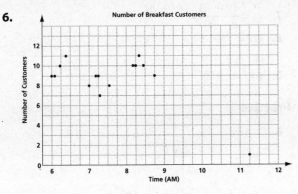

Number of Breakfast Customers

7. Answers will vary. Sample: The points in the scatter plot occur in clusters at approximately 6:15 AM, 7:15 AM, and 8:15 AM.

8. Answers will vary. Sample: The point representing this data is distant from the points in the clusters.

Practice

a. nonlinear

b. linear, outlier

c. cluster

Activity 24

1. Check students' work.

2. Check students' work.

3. Check students' work.

4. Answers may vary. Sample: They form a straight angle.

5. 180°, straight angle

6. Their sum is 180°

7. Check students' work.

8. 180°

9. 180°, straight angle

10. $m\angle 3, m\angle 3$

11. $m\angle 4$

Practice

a. 82°

b. 46°

c. 60°

d. 49°

e. 68°

f. 63°

g. 117°

Activity 25

1. Answers will vary. Sample: $2x + 4$

2. Answers will vary. Sample: $3x - 1$

3. Zero

4. True

Practice

a. $x = -2$

b. $x = 1$

c. $x = 8$

d. $x = -8$

e. $x = -3$

f. $x = 24$

Activity 26

1. Table: $\frac{3}{1}$, graph: $-\frac{2}{1}$

2. The absolute value of the slope of the graph of the function in the table is greater, so it's slope is steeper.

3. Table: $y = 3x$, graph: $y = -2x + 5$

4. The function represented by $y = 3x$ has the steeper graph.

5. Equation: -0.5, Graph: 0.25

6. The absolute value of the slope of the equation is greater, so it's graph is steeper.

7. $y = 0.25x + 3$

8. The function represented by $y = -0.5x + 3$ has the steeper graph.

Practice

a. Equation: $m = 8$, graph: $m = 1$, The function represented by the equation has the steeper graph.

b. Table: $m = -\frac{1}{2}$, graph: $m = \frac{1}{2}$; The absolute values of the slopes are equal, so the graphs are equally steep.

c. Company B, Company A charges at a rate of $25 per hour since $\frac{50}{2} = 25$. Company B charges $20 per hour since the slope of the graph is $\frac{20}{1}$.

Activity 27

1. 5, 8, 11, 14, 17, 20

2. $m = 3$, Answers will vary. Sample: (5, 17), (1, 5)

3. $b = 2$, Answers will vary. Sample: $2 = 3(0) + b$

4. $y = 3x + 2$

5. Answers will vary. Sample: (5, 15), (0, 5)

6. $m = 2$, $b = 5$, b represents beginning number of counters in the stack, $y = 2x + 5$

Practice

a. $y = 6x + 5$

b. $y = \frac{1}{4}x$

c. $y = -60x + 280$, Answers will vary. Sample: The slope is -60 which means that for every hour of travel the family has driven 60 miles. The y-intercept is (0, 280) which means that at the start of the trip the family was 280 miles from their destination.

Activity 28

1.

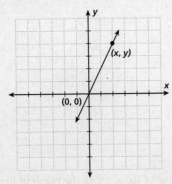

2. $m = \dfrac{(y - 0)}{(x - 0)} = \dfrac{y}{x}$

3. $mx = y$

4. $y = mx$

5. $(0, b)$

6.

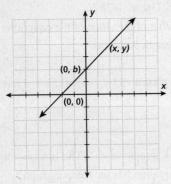

7. $m = \dfrac{(y - b)}{(x - 0)} = \dfrac{(y - b)}{x}$

8. $mx = y - b$

9. $mx + b = y$

10. $y = mx + b$

Practice

a. $y = \frac{1}{2}x + 1$

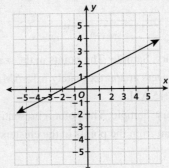

b. $y = -4x - 1$